SOME ASPECTS OF

INDIA'S PHILOSOPHICAL AND SCIENTIFIC HERITAGE

PHISPC MONOGRAPH SERIES ON
HISTORY OF PHILOSOPHY, SCIENCE
AND CULTURE IN INDIA

Editors

D.P. CHATTOPADHYAYA • RAVINDER KUMAR

---

1 Science, Philosophy and Culture in Historical Perspective

2 Some Aspects of India's Philosophical and Scientific Heritage

3 Mathematics, Astronomy and Biology in Indian Tradition: Some Conceptual Preliminaries

4 Language, Logic and Science in India: Some Conceptual and Historical Perspectives

SOME ASPECTS OF

INDIA'S PHILOSOPHICAL AND SCIENTIFIC HERITAGE

Contributors

PRAJIT K. BASU

SIBAJIBAN BHATTACHARYYA

MAHESH TIWARY

RAJA RAMANNA

KIREET JOSHI

PROJECT OF
HISTORY OF INDIAN SCIENCE, PHILOSOPHY
AND CULTURE

Sponsored by
INDIAN COUNCIL OF PHILOSOPHICAL RESEARCH

First published in 1995
by Professor Bhuvan Chandel, Member Secretary
for PHISPC, K 86 Hauz Khas Enclave, New Delhi 110 016

Distributed by
Munshiram Manoharlal Publishers Pvt. Ltd
54 Rani Jhansi Road, New Delhi 110 055

ISBN: 81-215-0687-5

Typeset at Tulika Print Communication Services, R-271 Greater Kailash I, New Delhi 110 048 and printed at Efficient Offset Printers, Shahzada Bagh Industrial Complex, Phase II, Delhi 110 035

Preface

The Project of History of Indian Science, Philosophy and Culture (PHISPC) that has been launched by the Indian Council of Philosophical Research, aided by Government of India and some other agencies, has made progress during the last few years. The main idea underlying the Project is to study the interconnection between Philosophy, Science and Technology as elements of the Culture of India. We have our political history, history of philosophy and history of science. Also, some attempts have been made to reconstruct our cultural history. It must be recognized here that the disciplines which are being distinctly named now as Science, Philosophy, etc. did not mean the same thing over the centuries in the past. Further, it should be admitted that the historical approach of the Project is not chronological or linear. Consciously it has been designed as conceptual. The hallmark of the Project is its interdisciplinarity.

The Project consists of an estimated ten volumes and some of the volumes are of two parts or more. Some very eminent historians, philosophers and classical scholars have already been positioned as Volume Editors. The contributors to the volumes are among the best available scholars in India.

This monograph and its companion publications provide glimpses of the comprehensive and interdisciplinary research work that has been undertaken by this Project (PHISPC). It is a critical exercise in rediscovering, recapturing and reinterpreting the heritage of India from a contemporary point of view. Like any other truly historical Project it has an implicit futural orientation.

EDITORS

Contents

1

Spreading of the (Al) Chemical Myth (Word): Scientific Explanation, Historiography of Indian Chemistry, and History of Philosophy

PRAJIT K. BASU

INTRODUCTION

In this essay my aim is two-fold. I want to raise general historiographical issues in the context of doing research in the history of Indian science, especially those which arguably arise in the history of Indian chemistry. In order to do that I shall look at two Indian alchemical texts of the mediaeval period in India. These two texts, *Rasārṇavakalpa* (hereafter *RNK*, a thirteenth century text, also influenced by Brahmanical tantric view), and *Rasa Ratna Samuccaya* (hereafter *RRS*, a late thirteenth, early fourteenth century iatrochemical text) offer a glimpse of the wealth of Indian alchemical/chemical/iatrochemical studies during the mediaeval period in India. Some preliminary analyses of the two texts also suggest new historiographical questions which need to be answered. Without answering them, I simply raise them in this essay. Second, I raise the question whether history of science, history of philosophy, and philosophy of science share an interface area for a fruitful investigation which can illuminate issues in these areas.[1]

This essay, viewed differently, has both a substantive aspect and a programmatic aspect. The substantive aspect involves offering a tentative understanding of the notion of explanation in some of the alchemical treaties of the mediaeval period. The programmatic aspect involves raising the questions concerning historiography of Indian chemistry during ancient and mediaeval periods, and thereby suggesting a route for research in that area.[2]

INDIAN ALCHEMY

In this section, I shall discuss some aspects of the Indian view of alchemy/chemistry. Historians of Indian alchemy and medicine have claimed that some of the salient features of the Indian alchemical view may be understood in the context of Sāṃkhya-Pātañjala philosophy. Although a discussion of the salient features of the Sāṃkhya-Pātañjala system may help in an understanding of the alchemical/chemical texts, I do not attempt it here because the texts do not suggest any overt dependence on this philosophical system. However, the texts are analysed within the broader context of this philosophical system to the extent the textual evidence suggests employment of such categories. For example, it was accepted that there were only five basic elements which gave rise to all the other chemical compounds. It was also accepted that these elements were 'property-bearing' elements. The notion of 'property-bearing' will also be explained. In the context of the general philosophical milieu in which these alchemical texts were written reflects acceptance of a view of causation which offered an account of material and efficient causes. Next, it is claimed that the philosophical view prevalent at the time of writing of these alchemical/chemical manuscripts also employs certain 'mechanistic' categories to explain chemical phenomena. A preliminary and thus sketchy understanding of explanation of phenomena in the context of the theory of causation and the theory of chemistry and that of matter is offered. It is extremely difficult to abstract a clear picture of what would be considered as an explanation in this chemical/alchemical context. Finally, I look into the possibility of chemical explanation being a special kind of reductive explanation. I also look at some important features of Indian alchemical texts. I start with a discussion of these features.

One of the most attractive features of the Indian alchemical texts is the adoption of some Indian mythological themes. The question is: was alchemy conforming to any particular tradition inspired by the idea and the symbolism of that time? Whether this form of expression is to be regarded as a rediscovery of the classical world is also to be established.

Those tales which the Greeks called myths, or more properly in origins, 'words', have been attributed to the 'result of the working of naive imagination upon the facts of experience'. In most cases the myth is an account of the deeds of a supernatural being, or

God, usually expressed in terms of primitive thought. It may have been an attempt to explain the relationship of man to the universe. The mythologies survive for various reasons. One of these is allegorization which has an ancient origin. It explains away the myth as an allegory, i.e., as a tale concealing deeper meaning, philosophical and moral, which must be withheld from those who are too ignorant and impious to use it properly.

The emphasis which symbolism placed upon the spiritual aspects of the art, taken together with the devaluation of the material possibilities of alchemy, removed alchemy from the hands of the gold maker. Alchemical work was also a spiritual quest to be followed only by adepts who truly understood nature. Nature was seen as active and animate. Thus, far from being passive and inert, dominated by forces external to them, individual bodies have their own sources of activities, whereby they set themselves in operation and perform specific acts. Since alchemy also expressed an organic view of nature in which no meaningful distinction between animate and inanimate existed, it perceived the whole of nature in organic terms. It understood processes that now we regard as entirely physical in terms of organic analogies. It held that metals/minerals grow in the earth and the non-efficacious metals/minerals when properly treated, yield gold. This is because non-precious (both in the sense of being a baser metal as compared to gold and also in the sense of being therapeutically less efficacious) metals are in some sense products of aborted natural process. Nature was seen as psychic. Projecting the mind onto nature, it understood the characteristic actions of bodies in similar terms. Bodies exercise influence on each other. Such a concept of natural action implied that agents are specific rather than general in their operation. The attraction of like for like was one of the characteristic ideas.

In Indian alchemy, there also underlies a world view to the effect that man (a microcosm) is the epitome of the universe (macrocosm). Both universe and man are manifestations of one and the same eternal spirit and the spirit and matter underlie both. Following the Sāṃkhya-Pātañjala system, both result from the evolution of *prakṛti*. At a more mundane or gross level, both are constituted of the same primary elements or principles. The same causal principles underlie phenomena in both the realms. Thus, *prakṛti* has eight aspects: *avyakta* (the unmanifested ground), *mahān* (ultimate experience), three fundamental *guṇas* (*sattva*, *rajas* and *tamas*), and three *ahaṅkāras* (guidance, energy, and inertia); and sixteen mutations—five organs of perception, five organs of action, the mind and the five *tanmātras*. The *pañcabhūtas* constitute all material substances. These *pañcabhūtas* have different properties. Thus, the earth principle gives mass, hardness, compactness, roughness, inertia, density, opacity, smell, and tactile sensations. The *ap* principle gives fluidity, viscosity, coldness, softness, unctuousness, and taste. The *tejas* principle gives visibility to objects, colours, periodicity of motion, digestion, anger, instantaneous response, courage, and the visual sensation. The *vāyu* principle gives perception by physical contact, all physical and physiological movements, pulsations, sense of lightness and the tactile sense. The *ākāśa* principle gives sound, porosity, bodily cavities, functional subdivisions of the bodily channels and tissues into finer and finer branches, and the sense of hearing. The medical as well as the alchemical texts of that time assumed that both the macrocosm and the microcosm are composed of all the five elements in different proportions and their properties result from the particular combination and composition of the different principles.[3]

There is yet another aspect of Indian alchemy which deserves mention. First, these texts are influenced by tantric way of life. Thus, we see reference to not only transmutation of base metals to gold but also bestowal of psychic powers on humans. This is referred to as *kāyasādhanā, dehasiddhi,* or *kāyakalpa*, a type of physical culture to become divine. This physical culture was performed by various means, like practice of *yoga* and *āsana*, and taking in of elixirs. This taking in elixirs was thought to help attain *siddhi.*[4]

The two texts that I consider here, though somewhat distinct, share two major alchemical goals, but the emphasis given on the therapeutic goal is more in *RRS* than in *RNK*, which emphasizes the efficacy of making gold. It does not mean that *RNK* did not have changing of the old to youthful state as one of its important goals. In fact, the emphasis was on transmutation of baser metals to gold because gold being the perfect metal is capable of being used as a drug both for restoration of youth and for curing diseases. *RNK* is an older text and primarily an alchemical text. It also contains information about ritual matters, intermingled with alchemical ideas. Roy and Subbarayappa point out that 'the style of expression with symbolic connotations of those parts are to some extent obscure and enigmatic'.[5] *RRS*, a well-known text of Indian alchemy/chemistry, ayurvedic pharmaceutics and therapeutics belongs to the later mediaeval period (thirteenth century AD). It deals mostly with drugs of mineral origin. Before I discuss a few interesting aspects of either text, I summarize below a few general points made by historians of chemistry regarding these texts.[6]

Indian alchemical tradition developed important procedures and techniques necessary to extend the use of mineral drugs. The development of pharmaceutical techniques had started from the time of *Caraka-Saṃhitā*. The text describes several procedures/techniques/operations which enhance the therapeutic properties of the original materials or induce in them certain new properties useful for the body. Following the text's terminology of *saṃskāra* (for the pharmaceutical processes and operations) one can say that 'these *saṃskāras* were responsible for *gunāntarādhāna* (inducing new or alternative properties) of the materials to be used for therapeutic purposes. Some examples of these techniques responsible for *guṇāntarādhāna* included *toya sannikarṣa* (contact of drug with liquid), *agni sannikarṣa* (contact of drug with fire), *toyagni sannikarṣa* (contact of drug with both liquid and fire), *saucha-śuddhikaraṇa* (purification/detoxication—external as well as internal), *manthana* (churning or grinding i.e., digestion of the particles), *bhāvanā* (addition of the same or different extractives with or without grinding), *vāsana* (flavouring). In addition to these procedures, the following factors were also admitted as the ones which were likely to influence the properties of the drugs during their processings: *deśa* (place of collection/preparation of drugs), *kāla* (time/season/duration of the collection/preparation), *bhājana* (influence of the containers during preparation/storage of the drugs), and *kāla prakarṣa* (effect of passage of time/long duration on the efficacy of the drug).[7]

The main concept of *Rasa-Śāstra* is to transform base/lower metals into noble/higher metals and to strengthen the body tissues and to maintain them in a fresh and healthy state so as to remove poverty, senility, diseases, and death from the world. Besides these, disease curing aspect is also included. Thus, *Rasa-Śāstras* were developed to achieve *lohavedha* (transformation of metals) and *dehavedha* (transformation of body for the prevention of ageing and diseases, and maintenance of positive health). Further, to achieve *dehavedha, Rasa-Śāstra* stressed more on *rasāyana* concept of āyurveda.[8] The *rasāyana* concept advises the ways and means by which one can achieve best quality of *rasādi dhātus* (body tissues) which in turn provide positive health to the body and prevent diseases and ageing, and thus sustain our body always in a healthy and youthful state. Historically, the *Rasa-Śāstras* developed the concept of *rasāyana.* Thus, from the eighth century AD, a number of metallic and mineral preparations were evolved and recognized to possess *rasāyana* property which on continuous internal use would maintain body health, prevent ageing and the onset of diseases. If required, these may also be used for curing diseases. It must also be mentioned that in *Rasa-Śāstra,* the metals and the minerals are also termed as *dhātus* and *upadhātus* because of their specific role in biological systems i.e., these can sustain body tissues by supplementing some of the essential elements to the tissues, whose deficiency causes many undesired problems/diseases in the body.[9]

In the *Rasa-Śāstra* and *rasa* therapy, the use of mineral drugs, especially of mercury and sulphur (the most basic materials) was recognized. It was also recognized that these drugs were toxic. In order to reduce or remove their toxicity, a number of *śodhana* measures were developed. 'These include grinding of such drugs with vegetable extractives and with other acidic or alkaline liquids, their heating and dipping in various liquids, or their boiling, fusion, sublimation etc.; measures which in turn remove washable/soluble and/or volatile impurities of the drugs of mineral origin. Sometimes some organic/inorganic materials are added either in traces or in large amounts to these substances which helped either in their detoxication or in their potentiation.'[10]

By *mārana* process the drugs of mineral origin are converted to a fine ash form, suitable for systemic absorption. To achieve this, the drugs of mineral origin are first subjected to *bhāvanā* (grinding with some vegetable extractives and acidic liquids) and then to *puṭapāka* (heating through scheduled heating system) several times. With the development of *Rasa-Śāstra,* more such processes were developed. For example, in the case of *abhraka,* the method of *dhānyābhraka* is mentioned in between *śodhana* and *mārana* processes. In the same way, an intermediary procedure known as *jārana* was developed for *nāga, vaṅga* and *yaśada* with a view to convert these low melting/easily fusing metals into a powder form. They also developed various kinds of *mārana* drugs for increasing or decreasing the efficacy for the drugs being converted to ashes. They mentioned that if mercury or its compounds are used as the *mārana* drugs before employing the actual *mārana* process, the finished products will be of a very high quality. In this method, though mercury is not present in the final product, still it is claimed that the *bhasma* so prepared may be inducted with certain special properties and thus the product becomes more effective than the products made by other methods. *Mārana* with vegetable extractives is second best because the *bhasma* would be devoid of the properties of mercury and sulphur. *Sattvapātana* is another important process which helps the release of *satva* (metallic content) of a mineral or a rock. *Druti* is another important process in which metals are converted into a *druta* (stable liquefied state).[11] A cursory glance at *RNK* seems to point out that they employed various kinds of processes to purify, and extract required materials. There are at least thirty or more different kinds of processes which are mentioned in *RNK*.

Mercury having been *mūrcchita* (compounded) destroys diseases, having been solidified/bound/fixed provides emancipation and having been converted to ashes makes the person immortal; hence there is no better compassionate substance than mercury. One can achieve liberation only by achieving perfect knowledge, and the knowledge is possible by continuous practice and the same is possible only by a sound physique. No *rasāyana,* either of vegetable or metallic origin is capable of making the body physically sound because these themselves are unstable, as they can be burnt, moistened and dried.[12]

Although the *Rasa-Śāstras* have been discussed to a large extent, the *rasāyana karma, loha karma* or *rasa karma* aspects were not completely neglected. Thus, we see that there are discussions or mention of substances which are efficacious for *loha karma* or *rasa karma.* This we see especially in *RRS* which was a late thirteenth or early fourteenth century iatrochemical text. Similar emphasis on *rasāyana karma* is seen in most of the other iatrochemical texts.

The properties of mercury described in *RRS* show that there are five types of mercury (or *rasa*). The descriptions imply that *rasa* is an agent. It performs certain activities by virtue of its power and is in liquid form. Also, depending upon its situation, it can be associated with the motion of soul and attain *jīvagatī.* Hence, mercury is also called *jīva.* If we consider the therapeutic and alchemical properties of the eight *rasas,* we find that the following important features stand out. First, these, when treated with 'proper' herbal juices, achieve some special properties. For example, these can 'destroy' various kinds of diseases. Since the most important goal of a *Rasa-Śāstra* is to provide knowledge about *rasas*, their properties, their efficacies in maintaining health of humans, so that humans can attain *dharma, artha, kāma,* and *mokṣa,* the knowledge that is provided in *RRS* or any other alchemical text is a list of various substances and the methods of making them (more) efficacious by treating them with various herbal/vegetable plants. The underlying method assumes that one has to experiment and then determine what are the important substances which achieve the goals. An analysis of the text reveals e.g., that mercury having consumed *abhraka* as a solute is good for both *loha karma* and *rasāyana karma.* There is also a list of several processes with *abhraka* including *satva.* In only some of the cases the properties of the products are mentioned. This seems to lend credence to the belief that at least some, if not all, of these different products were tested for *rasāyana karma* adequacy. This experimentation and determination is also guided by some method. For example, consider how the author in *RRS* attempts to correlate the alchemical uses of *abhraka* with that of its colour. White *abhraka* is used to prepare silver, while red *abhraka* is used for dyeing, and yellow is used for gold making. This recommendation perhaps assumes the following understanding—at least some properties of a product are dependent upon the properties of its constituents. The colour property e.g., can be transferred by the component substance to its compound. Consider again, the case of another *rasa, śilajatu.* The first interesting point is that it is of two types—*sasatva* and *nissatva,* i.e., with therapeutic power and without therapeutic power. Thus, it is the presence or absence of *satva* in a substance which determines whether at all the substance has any kind of power. Second, the *nissatva* variety is still *śilajatu* although of the inefficacious kind. Thus, its nature as *śilajatu* is not changed although it lacks a certain therapeutic property. We also see from the text that *śilajatu* obtained from the gold containing mountain rock is reddish in colour. It is the best *rasāyana. Śilajatu* obtained from silver containing mountain rock can cure some diseases, while that obtained from the mountain containing copper rocks has no therapeutic power. This seems to imply that the circumstance of this *rasa* both in terms of its specific location (and hence in terms of the process of its production) and/or interaction with the specific environment in that location plays a significant role in determining its therapeutic property. Gold containing rocks must play a role in making *śilajatu* the best *rasāyana*. The presence of gold either facilitates the process or takes an active role in the process. Since gold is the goal of alchemical research, it seems that it would play an active role in the process. Since silver is the next best metal, its effect is much less. The question is why is it that the circumstances provided by silver containing mountain is less efficacious. I suggest that it is because the process which gives *śilajatu* its therapeutic property is either aborted or modified in this case. The circumstances play a causal role in inhibiting the process leading the said substance to obtaining the best therapeutic property. Similar example of aborted process is mentioned in *RNK*.[13] Thus, gold obtained from a base metal, treated with mercury prepared with the juice of *trnausadhis*, is up to the half way level as attained in the case of a total (perfect) conversion. Before I consider what interesting philosophical implication these examples have, I want to mention a few more interesting examples.

We also see that mercury prepared in various ways has different powers of transmutation. Some preparations enable mercury to convert base metals million times its weight into gold, or convert it by mere touch, or by showing the mercury to the metal. Or gold prepared in some way can bestow *dharma, artha, kāma,* and *mokṣa,* while prepared in another way, it is less efficacious and can help attain only *dharma, artha* and *kāma*.[14]

We next briefly consider another substance (discussed in some detail in *RRS*), sulphur. The description of the mythological origin of sulphur and its properties reflects the belief in *Śiva-Pārvatī* union at the cosmic level. Thus, mercury and sulphur union at the microcosmic level is analogically the same kind of union at the macrocosmic level between *Śiva* and *Pārvatī*. Hence, sulphur also has a very superior *rasāyana* property. This kind of analogical reasoning plays an important role in not only ascribing an important therapeutic role to some substances but also in justifying or substantiating the alchemists' belief in the (therapeutic) efficacy of some over the other. The archetype of *Śiva-Pārvatī* union at the cosmic level reinforces the desirability of the union of mercury and sulphur at the micro level.

The examples that we discussed above regarding the production of different kinds of *śilajatu* or gold seem to raise the following plausible explanation for the difference in the final product, given the difference in circumstances. Suppose it is held that a universal cause, U, is causally responsible for bringing about the production of both kinds of *śilajatu,* say S1 and S2. One way in which one could explain that would be to appeal to different environmental circumstances. The environmental circumstance E1, along with U is causally responsible for the production of S1, while the environmental circumstance E2, along with U, is causally responsible for the production of S2. We need to remind ourselves that S2 is the product of an aborted (modified) process which otherwise would have given us S1. This means that E2 played an important causal role to help abort the process. The reason one holds that the process was aborted is due to the fact that the product (S2) of the aborted process can be transmuted to S1 by another process. While this may broadly be in accordance with the Sāṃkhya account of causation, the alchemists might not have strictly followed this view. It is not clear whether they wanted to posit the first material or efficient cause to explain the production of different kinds of *rasas.* In fact, one may want to refute this thesis because one may claim that this involves positing a first cause, U. In order to look at this refutation let me first make explicit the thesis (of universal power) that one is trying to refute. The thesis has two parts: (1) the cause of *rasas* is a certain power, which is one in all things; (2) the power varies greatly in proportion to the material that receives it and the circumstances that the material is in; hence, *rasas* with different therapeutic properties are produced in different places. It appears that this thesis is extremely plausible. I will first raise a plausible objection and then go on to evaluate it. The objection is that we are looking for *immediate* material or efficient causes existing in the material and transmuting it. And if the above claim is correct, then, once we know the universal cause producing *rasas* we should know the cause of everything that can be produced. This is because the effect of the environment (E) modifies the power of the universal cause such that the process is carried through in one case, while it is aborted in the other. We know that the motion and power of the elemental bodies is the ultimate cause of things. But these perhaps are acting causes in a different sense, since they have nothing in common with the materials of the things that can be produced. But, in accordance with the proper methods of natural science, we should look for causes appropriate to their effects, and especially for the material and whatever transmutes it.

The above refutation can be systematically expressed as follows:

(1) The first cause for action and movement is the power of the elemental bodies.
(2) We need *immediate* causes, existing in the material and transmuting it.
(3) If a universal power is the *immediate* cause for the production of *rasas*, then once we know this cause we can know the *immediate* cause for producing anything.
(4) The consequent of the conditional statement in (3) is false because we know that the universal power is different from natural (immediate) causes.
(5) A universal power is not the *immediate* cause.

One can also object that a universal power is an equivocal cause. But in natural science we are looking for univocal cause. Hence, the universal power cannot be an *immediate* cause for the production of non-precious metals or inefficacious *rasas*. Let us look at the first argument. It appears that the most crucial premise in the argument is premise (4). There are several arguments for establishing this premise. Before we go into that let us explain what one may mean by *immediate* and remote (efficient?) causes. Thus, we say a man is healthy because the physician healed him. The physician healed him by the art of healing that he possesses. The former is the *immediate* and the latter is the remote (efficient?) cause.

One way to argue for premise (4) is dependent upon the second argument outlined above. This argument depends upon the notion of causes acting in the equivocal sense. This in turn depends upon the general metaphysical belief that nature is that seat of power from which the powers pour into the material. Since the same nature produces various kinds of things, it uses other causal agents instrumentally. The assumption here is that we should look for causes acting univocally. One thinks that only the knowledge of these kinds of causes which are appropriate to their natures are useful in natural philosophy. Thus, an explanation of a phenomenon is good on the first level if one posits an immediate (efficient?) cause in a univocal sense for an effect. But there are several kinds of phenomena in nature. To explain these as effects under a general causal principle would require a deeper and broader explanation. Thus the causal principle invoked has to be equivocal in sense. An analogy may help to understand the situation better. Knowledge generically helps one to build or make many things. But only specific knowledge of healing in a physician makes him a physician.

A physician can be said to heal by knowledge. But more specifically, a physician can be said to heal by the knowledge of the art of healing that he possesses. If we say knowledge healed this man and similarly knowledge built this building, then one might think that if we possess the knowledge that healed this man, we can make this building by the same knowledge. But this of course is not correct. Thus premise (4) is established beyond any reasonable doubt since the power that causes one *rasa* is not the same power that causes another *rasa*. These two causes or powers are different so long as these are immediate (efficient?) causes. That the alchemists confronted this tension between search for univocal and equivocal causes, although perhaps unknowingly, is obvious and will be hinted below when we discuss their methodology and plausible modes of scientific explanations suggested by their work. The tension was aggravated because the theoretical explanations of chemical phenomena lagged far behind their practical explanation. I now turn to that aspect in the next section.

METHODOLOGY AND EXPLANATORY SCHEMA IN (AL) CHEMICAL WORKS

At the time when these treatises were written, the traditional explanations of the (al)chemists could be interpreted as follows. Mundane objects were made up of 'principles' or elements which *conferred* properties upon the materials of which they were constituents. Such a mode of explanation would be congenial to a chemist/alchemist/iatrochemist with empirical interests, suspicious or unaware of too much theory. Consider what a theoretical explanation of a chemical or therapeutic or alchemical property would be like. From the point of view of Sāṃkhya-Patañjala system, the explanation is very complex. Thus, for example, the 'isomeric' modes of each *mahābhūta* have specific colour or taste due to their structure, i.e. the arrangement of their *paramāṇus*, and the various properties of the compounds arise from the collocation in unequal proportion of the different forces latent in the *paramāṇus* of the component substances. A new substance may arise by the interplay of energies within the system of any given substance, in the absence of any action from without. New qualities like new substances are only readjustments of the old, and continual changes are going on by spontaneous disintegration and recombination.[15] It is extremely unclear what practical information in terms of getting an idea of a univocal cause can be obtained from such deep theoretical explanation. Also, the practicing (al)chemists had a real need for explanations of the phenomena/properties such as colour, efficacy in curing certain kinds of diseases, or in prevention of diseases, or promoting health, to name a few. Among the (al)chemists, explanations in terms of the definite material substances would be favoured more on the practical ground. To say that the cause of colour lay in the specific principles would be to offer the prospect of *useful* explanations of a range of (al)chemical phenomena. Or to say that the efficacy of certain kinds of drugs is due to the presence of a certain kind of substance or principle would help prepare and use that drug. The explanatory schema that this view suggests is as follows.

Let a compound C have properties P1 and P2. Let that compound be decomposed to determine its constituents. Let these constituents be E1 and E2. The properties P1 and P2 can now be explained in terms of the properties of E1 and E2. The explanation will proceed as follows. Either E1 or E2 or both E1 and E2 have the properties P1 and P2. These properties (P1 and P2) are essential properties of E1 (or of E2 or of both E1 and E2). Therefore, the whole has a property because the part has that property. Thus, to take an example, C has the property of being solid. One of the constituents of C is earth. The earth has the property of being solid. So, the property of being solid is conferred to the whole compound C. This kind of explanation appears to be a weak form of reductive explanation. For in this kind of explanation, the whole has a property by virtue of its part having the same property. This of course does not mean that the whole has a property because every physical part of it has that property. Thus, the explanation of why this substance is therapeutically efficacious is not given by appealing to the therapeutic efficacy of its physical parts but by appealing to the therapeutic property of, say, one of its constituents. The therapeutic property that the compound has is a property of the whole and isotropic and independent of the mass of the body.

Interestingly enough, the alchemists/iatrochemists of that time also allowed that every compound has some specific property that distinguishes it from its constituents. However, they are silent as to what kind of explanation one can give for such properties. One might think that sometimes C exemplifies a property not merely because the constituent has that property but also because the constituent is in a particular physical state. This physical state is described in terms of motion and degree of tenuity of the particles of the constituent. Thus, the physical state helps to make the property manifest. The physical state of a constituent can hasten or slow down a particular process of combination or resolution. The question then is, can a substance have the chemical property of reacting in some specified way, which becomes observable only when that substance is in a particular physical state? It is unclear what the answer could be. Now, how is that property to be explained? I think one would claim that the constituent has the potential with respect to such a particular state of having that property. The reason that I expect such an answer to be appropriate is because first, fire or air or even water can act as instruments. It is true that water is a principle. But water as an instrument, much like other instruments, does not change the essences of the constituents. Second, the alchemists use dispositional property, like being disposed to be solid etc. Thus, it would seem very reasonable that a dispositional property needs to be understood in terms of potentiality.

However, the question remains whether this reductionism, if it really is a reductionist programme, is a trivial kind of reductionism. I think it is not. Because it seems these (al)chemists need to give us an account of the dispositional properties of the 'property-bearing' elements. And this account needs to be given in the context of their theory of elements and theory of causation. One way to account for these properties is to invoke the notions of actuality and potentiality. These concepts are conceptually connected with the concept of motion. Thus, what is entirely in potentiality is not moved yet; what is already in complete actuality, is not moved but what has already been moved; what is partly in potentiality and partly in actuality i.e., what is intermediate between pure potentiality and pure actuality is moved.

It appears that the explanation schema in the alchemical writings we considered follows a very weak reductive strategy in which the property of a compound is explained by positing the constituents which make up the compound has that property. Thus, the whole has a property because its part has that property. However, it is unclear how the dispositional properties are explained. It is also not obvious how we can explain the specific property of a compound which sets that compound apart from its constituents. In fact explanations of the last two kinds of properties may be strong reductive explanations with property-identities. But I am not sure. It is possible that these works can be understood completely in terms of mediaeval theory of causation and five principles of elements and the theory of motion. We need to remember that for the philosophers/chemists of the mediaeval period, causes are always things. A thing has a particular power to do what it does. It may use its power by itself or if it is an instrument, its power is used by an agent. Thus water has power to move certain things. But it exercises its power only as an instrument under certain conditions. Or a knife has the power to carve things. But it exercises its power only through an agent who uses that knife to carve, say a piece of marble. And I am not sure if a chemist would like to ask why is it that knife, as knife, has the power to carve.

I want to close this section with the following comments. The exercise above involved outlining some of the salient features of the two alchemical texts and a subsequent attempt to abstract an account of scientific explanation raises some important methodological questions. First, does history of science has any role to play in doing a more fruitful history of philosophy? Second, does one need to do history of science to illuminate issues in philosophy of science? I will not attempt to discuss the answer to the second question except to point out that my inclination is to answer the question in the affirmative. In proposing an answer to the first question, I start by pointing out that an important activity of philosophy is taken to be a painstaking clarification of the fundamental concepts and questions. How does history of philosophy fit in this schema? One answer would be that history of philosophy can be seen as a progressive clarification of the questions that have been raised since the ancient days and evaluations of various answers to these questions. Though this answer is innocuous enough, it is not and cannot be the correct account. One would like to know whether philosophy at different times raises the same questions. For example, did the philosophers of one period mean the same thing by an explanation of a phenomenon as the philosophers of a somewhat previous era? The question is hardly rhetorical. It is not *a priori* given to us that the philosophers of different times separated by hundreds of years understood the same thing by the same question, or could evaluate an answer to a question by applying the criteria which need not have remained unchanged. If they did not, then their answers to the questions cannot be evaluated by appealing to an eternal criteria of evaluation. And if they did, then it is a historically contingent fact and has to be established by historical research and scholarship. Even then the criteria employed for evaluations could be different. More likely, the nature and type of philosophical questions raised at any time would reflect the cultural/intellectual milieu of the period. This *a posteriori* aspect of history of philosophy thus raises the following question about the analyses of alchemical texts provided above. The notion of explanation that was abstracted from the analysis may be an answer to a question raised in the context of the present philosophy of science. Did the alchemists raise questions about explanation? In the next section, while discussing the problems of historiography of Indian chemistry, it is mentioned that the alchemists might have implicitly viewed their work in the tradition of elaborating a *prayojana śāstra*, without feeling the need for developing any methodological prescription which would be philosophically defencible. In that context, the attempts to prepare substances with specific properties with ease might have provided the overriding consideration for experimenting, elaborating, and systematizing the already established body of knowledge. Questions that concerned deep theoretical explanation of phenomena or properties were simply not raised in this narrow context.

HISTORIOGRAPHY OF CHEMISTRY

In this section, I want to raise some issues concerning the historiography of Indian chemical traditions. Even in the western historiographic tradition, chemistry occupies a subsidiary position in the historiographical hierarchy. Only a few historians are interested in history of chemistry or of alchemy. If we compare that with the ever increasing amount of work on history of physics, or of biology, we find that chemistry has indeed been the neglected discipline. Added to that is the apology that chemistry as a discipline had to offer by attempting to delineate itself from alchemy (tantric work in the Indian context).

History of Indian chemistry (or alchemy) has suffered as much as the history of western chemistry because of the Indian chemists' and historians' preoccupation with two views. First was (and to some extent still is) to understand Indian chemical works or traditions mainly from the point of view of the present knowledge of chemistry—more particularly that of atomism. The historians of Indian chemistry were, or still are, very much preoccupied with chemical atomism of the West. Hence, what goes on in the name of presenting, justifying, and legitimizing Indian chemistry of the ancient or mediaeval times is an elaboration of various philosophical systems e.g., the Sāṃkhya-Patañjala system or the Nyāya-Vaiśeṣika system (especially Kaṇāda's view), or the Buddhist view, or the Jain view of atomism or theory of matter. We are also given accounts of different theories of causation offered by these different schools, the account of explanation, and an account of certain allegedly chemical concepts e.g., chemical compound or mixture. Although I have not the slightest reason to claim that these exercises are not important for a better understanding of Indian chemical/alchemical systems, still what I find extremely problematic is that such exercises seem to be the only kind of legitimate historiography that we are offered. What is not recognized is that this historiography has two major inadequacies. First, it is centred around the western concept of modern chemistry--especially of atomism. Second, it borrows, by virtue of its acceptance of chemical atomism of the West as a provider of perspective, the categories of western science (in this case, of chemistry) and applies it to a product of a different cultural milieu.

The other significant drawback, which follows from the presentist historiography, affecting the Indian chemical historiography, is the temptation to present a modern chemical analysis of some of the chemical/metallurgical artefacts, or a listing of various chemical operations. The reason for presenting such a list is unclear unless we want to point out that Indians in the ancient period were aware of or had the knowledge of certain techniques or perhaps the knowledge of certain materials which the Europeans did not. The question, however, remains as to how or why presentation of such results should or would add to our understanding of Indian chemistry. After all we are not attempting to prove that our ancestors had some knowledge, in the presentist sense, which, by the fall of Grace or whatever, was lost in the dark ages. If that is what we are trying to do, then this is hardly any basis of sound historiographical exercise. This is because we cannot legitimately claim that the operations listed in the (al)chemical texts mean the same as the operations that we find in modern chemistry textbooks. To claim that an *amla* substance is an acidic material is to run aground with historical sensitivity which required to understand the past in its own terms. Simply put, a history that does not disown its presentist categories distorts the past and is no history at all. Lest I be thought as someone who is fighting a straw person, consider Professor P. Ray's *History of Chemistry in Ancient and Medieval India,* still the only major work on the history of Indian chemistry. This work is an edited version of Acharya P.C. Ray's two volume work entitled *History of Hindu Chemistry.* The actual reasons for Acharya Ray's motivations for this research, which might have included resurgence of aspirations of Indian nationalism do not need to be discussed here. But Professor Ray's edition reflects the worries of a chemist trained in western science. Hence, we are told, e.g., while discussing tantric (alchemical) literature, that this literature contains descriptions of important chemical phenomena. A cursory glance of the choice of (translated) *ślokas* printed in the book reflects the inclination of the author concerning what constitutes important chemical phenomena. These phenomena are those which could be understood from the point of view of modern chemistry. Problems of a different sort arise when we look at Professor B.N. Seal's work.[16] There we have an elaborate philosophical account of various philosophical systems. This is important no doubt, but is also inadequate. Because it does not attempt to even start to bridge the gap between alchemy and these philosophical accounts. It fails to discuss Indian alchemy with a seriousness the subject deserves. Of course, there are exceptions, such as Joshi's pioneering translation of *RRS* and Roy and Subbarayappa's translation of *RNK* (although the text does not include the first fifty-two *ślokas* for reasons that are unclear).

I conclude that the historiography of Indian chemistry thus has suffered doubly. It has suffered because the presentist historiography was imposed in analysing chemical/alchemical texts. It has also suffered because the western concept of chemical atomism, with its conceptual baggage, provided the Archimedean point for our historical research into Indian chemistry. This dominance has primarily led us to look for those strands in the Indian chemical tradition which could be interpreted as, or which are, a species of atomism. Instead of succumbing to this historiography, I want to raise and consider a plausible and viable alternative which might redress some of these problems. This involves, following Christie and Golinski (see note 2), considering 'the question of the nature of chemistry as a historical practice'. When we talk of chemistry, we of course, want to consider the subject matter of chemistry, modes of investigation in chemistry, delineation of chemistry from other branches of knowledge as something which is historically contingent and not given to us *a priori*. It needs to be understood that the practice of chemistry both in terms of production of material objects or of knowledge claims and in terms of dissemination of that knowledge is socially and culturally governed. Thus, human beings play an important role in producing such cultural artefacts as specific chemical objects or specific chemical texts. Viewed from this perspective, the role of philosophical systems is not to be belittled but may not be given undue prominence as well. The roles of epistemology, metaphysics, or theology etc. are to be taken into account but only to the extent these (contingently) inform the cultural practice called alchemical/chemical work. By following this approach, one avoids the possibility of subsuming history under a specific philosophical schema. Consider one of the thematic centres of the proposed historiography. It is known that there were many chemical/alchemical manuscripts written between the ninth and sixteenth centuries. What do these manuscripts serve as? These, I claim, following Christie and Golinksi (see note 2) are 'the cultural artefacts of that specific period'. They embody a certain understanding of nature. But more importantly, these texts serve some important purposes including didactic purpose.[17] It is an open question, one to be resolved by historical research and scholarship, whether writing such texts was a part of a long tradition. To answer that question, one has to ask whether there was a formal tradition of disseminating alchemical/chemical knowledge, what kinds of historical conditions helped preserve that tradition, whether the manuscripts of the texts were circulated, and among whom were these circulated, thereby providing 'a further means of cultural transmission'. Also, question can be raised whether the didactic form imposed any constraint in not only presenting the material but also in conceptualizing the body of (al)chemical knowledge. It may also turn out to be the case that there were varieties of formal traditions. Consider the introduction of *RRS*. The author gives credit to a long list of people in compiling this treatise. What purpose did this particular text serve if it was a mere compilation of some already known alchemical processes? Even if it did provide some new methods, (in this case it actually did), was it supposed to pass on this information for posterity, or was it supposed to be used as a text for didactic purposes only? As pointed out before, Subbarayappa mentions in one line in his introduction to *RNK* that it also served didactic purposes. He is completely silent regarding who taught, and to whom, where was it taught, what did the students subsequently do, was it the only text that was taught, or was it one among many? Answers to these questions are crucial for an understanding of the nature of Indian chemistry/alchemy.

The next question deals with the method employed in writing the text. An analysis of the ordering of the subject matter of the text should give us insight regarding what constitutes important chemical practices and important chemical concepts. Given that most, if not all, of the alchemical/chemical texts were written to serve specific medical goals of providing good health, which in turn was necessary to achieve liberation, and even that objects from mineral, vegetable, and animal kingdoms were mixed together and processed reflects a lack of hierarchy from the point of view of efficacy of medicines produced from species of one particular kingdom. Yet another question which needs to be raised and answered is the role of natural philosophy in informing these texts. What I have in mind is not so much imposing one philosophical system or another on the text but to worry what motivated some of these writers/alchemists/practitioners of medicine to assume an analogy between the working of the cosmos (at the macro level) and the human body (the microcosm). How the working of the human body was modelled after the working of the cosmos needs to be explored. I will raise another important question before I end this section. In many alchemical/chemical texts we are given an account of a *rasaśāla* where all the operations of *rasa* are performed. Now, there are specific instructions as to how it is to be set up, and what operations are to be performed here. Joshi's suggestions notwithstanding a deeper understanding of the geography of the *rasaśāla* will illuminate our understanding of the analogy between macro(cosm)–micro(cosm). It is a place where elixirs are prepared. These elixirs either help give a long life or transmute a metal other than gold into gold. Thus, the cosmic power is localized in the specific substances produced in a specific way in a specific place. The role of metaphysical world views in setting up the *rasaśāla* is something that must have played an important part in practising alchemy.

Finally, I want to briefly raise the point that alchemy/chemistry of the period we are talking about here, is also to be understood as *prayojana śāstra.* This only means that these have some definite goals which are mundane and are not necessarily developed with the esoteric goal of providing a deeper understanding of nature. As a result, most practitioners might not have felt the need to justify it by appealing to a specific philosophical system. The teleological concern for ensuring the health of a person which in turn will help him/her to achieve *dharma, artha, kāma,* and *mokṣa* is the primary concern. To that extent it shares its concerns with āyurveda. But it differs from āyurveda to the extent that it also aims at transmuting base metals to gold, although to achieve the primary goals. And it visualizes the world as a seat of power, and humans as the microcosms of the powers in the world. Seen from this perspective, a serious study of Indian alchemy should provide the conceptual apparatus underlying the activity, both in terms of its practices, and knowledge claims. If the discussion in the previous section is any indication, question regarding the problematics and hard to get at notion of e.g., scientific explanation perhaps have to be raised and understood in a very different way from the way it is raised and answered in the western analytic tradition.

NOTES AND REFERENCES

1. My discussion in this essay has been strongly influenced by two programmatic papers. These are D.P. Chattopadhyaya's 'On the Nature of Interconnections between Science, Technology, Philosophy and Culture', *Project of History of Indian Science, Philosophy and Culture,* and Ravinder Kumar's 'Reflections on the Proposal: A History of Science, Philosophy and Culture in Indian Civilization', *Project of History of Indian Science, Philosophy and Culture.* I also wish to acknowledge the keen interest shown in this work by Professor N.C. Nigam, Director, Indian Institute of Technology, Delhi.
2. My indebtedness to J.R.R. Christie and J. Golinski's essay 'Spreading of the World', *History of Science,* 22, 1982, pp. 235–66, is acknowledged. The title of my essay reflects my indebtedness.
3. R.C. Majumdar, 'Medicine', in D.M. Bose, S.N. Sen, and B.V. Subbarayappa (eds.), *A Concise History of Science in India,* Indian National Science Academy, New Delhi, 1971, pp. 213–74; see especially pp. 228–31.
4. M. Roy, and B.V. Subbarayappa, (trs. and eds.), *Rasārnavakalpa,* Indian National Science Academy, New Delhi, 1976, pp. 3–4.
5. Ibid., p. 2.
6. I rely for my discussion here mainly on two references cited above and on articles by B.V. Subbarayappa, 'Chemical Practices and Alchemy', in A Concise History of Science in India, Indian National Science Academy, New

6. I rely for my discussion here mainly on two references cited above and on articles by B.V. Subbarayappa, 'Chemical Practices and Alchemy', in *A Concise History of Science in India,* Indian National Science Academy, New Delhi, 1971, pp. 274–338; see especially pp. 309–38; and by D. Joshi, (tr. and ed.), *Rasa Ratna Samuccaya, Indian Journal of History of Science,* No. 22, 1987, No. 24, 1989, and No. 27, 1992, (published as supplement). See especially No. 22, 1987 supplement, pp. 1–17.
7. Ibid.
8. For a somewhat different interpretation of the concept of *rasāyana,* see Roy and Subbarayappa cited in note 2. However, Majumdar's view is similar to that of Joshi.
9. See note 7.
10. Ibid.
11. Ibid.
12. Ibid.
13. That the alchemists held the view that circumstances can abort or modify natural processes is borne out from textual evidence. See especially, *RNK,* pp. 107–10.
14. *RNK,* See pp. 64, 66, 72 and 74.
15. B.N. Seal, *The Positive Sciences of the Hindus,* Motilal Banarsidass, New Delhi, 1958. See especially pp. 23–53.
16. Ibid.
17. See Roy and Subbarayappa cited in note 2, p. 1. They acknowledge that the style of writing reflects the didactic nature of other Sanskrit texts but do not follow up the suggestion.

2

The Emergence of the Person: Some Indian Themes and Theories

SIBAJIBAN BHATTACHARYYA

INTRODUCTION

There are different philosophical theories about the nature of the person; for example, according to some the concept of the person is logically prior to the concepts of the body and the mind of the person; according to others the person is a combination of the body and the mind; and according to a third group of philosophers, the person is identified with the mind or the self which is simple, a monad. There is, however, a radically different type of philosophers according to whom our consciousness of ourselves as persons is a mistake. Really, we are not persons at all. The person is constructed out of what is impersonal. There are two different types of this theory. According to Hume, Robert Nozick, Derek Parfit, as also in Yogācāra Buddhism, the reality is a succession of momentary mental states. In Advaita Vedānta, on the other hand, consciousness is eternal, but universal and impersonal. One main problem of this type of philosophy is to explain how the awareness of individual selves can be founded on impersonal consciousness.

THE METHODOLOGY OF STUDY

The problem here is to explain how we are to account for our awareness of our selves. It is usual to treat this question as the question of what we believe ourselves to be. Yet we do not believe ourselves to be the same person, the same individual, all the time. When we are awake we identify ourselves mostly with our bodies and consider ourselves as embodied. But this identification with our body is forgotten when we dream that we are children, giants or whatever. When I dream that I am a child I forget my identity in waking state and identify myself with the child in the dream. McCawley's paradoxical example, 'I dreamt that I was Brigitte Bardot and that I kissed me' clearly brings out not merely the logical difficulty of cross-reference but also the psychological, epistemological and ontological difficulties in explaining dream experience. It is also clear that I may identify myself with someone for some time, and with someone else in a different dream. In deep dreamless sleep, again, I do not have any awareness of my identity. The problem here is to decide whether to base a philosophy of the self exclusively on waking experience, or also to consider dream experience and deep dreamless sleep.

It may be argued here that waking experience alone matters and so a philosophical theory of the self as person ought to be based on the evidence of waking experience alone.

This sort of consideration has its limitations. To argue in this way would be similar to argue in epistemology that veridical perceptions alone matter and that, therefore, an epistemological theory of perception should be exclusively based upon veridical perceptions ignoring aberrations like illusions, hallucinations etc. Even though it be granted that most of the time our perceptions are vertical, and only rarely illusory, still philosophical theory of perception cannot be based on veridical perception alone. Similarly, a philosophical theory of the self cannot be based on the evidence of waking experience only, but has to take into account dreams and dreamless sleep. It is a peculiarity of Indian philosophical systems that a philosophy of the self is based on waking experience, dream and also deep dreamless sleep.

There is, however, a puzzle of identifying the dreaming subject with the empirical subject on waking from the dream. McCawley, gives this paradoxical example: 'I dreamt that I was Brigitte Bardot and that I kissed me'. So long as the dream lasted McCawley was Brigitte Bardot; in his dream the person that was McCawley was a different person; when identifying himself with Brigitte Bardot in the dream he could not continue to identify himself also with the person with whom he identified himself in the waking state. This means that even in dream he could not identify himself with two persons. One can identify oneself with one person in a dream and with another on waking from the dream. When McCawley wakes up from the dream, he identifies himself with the person whom Bardot kissed in the dream; but then he no longer is Bardot.

But if the dreaming subject is identical with the empirical subject on waking, when McCawley dreamt that he as Bardot kissed McCawley who he is on waking, then, as a matter of fact, in the dream he kissed himself! Professor Kalidas Bhattacharya has denied the possibility of such identification of the dreaming subject with the empirical subject on waking. Just as correcting an illusory perception is the realization not merely of the unreality of the object perceived (the snake), but also of the seeing of the snake, so also is the case in the dream. (i) The 'I' who dreamt is rejected as being identical with the 'I' in waking consciousness. I often am not ready to recognize the identity of the dreaming subject with me. (ii) The other persons in the dream are recognized as unreal on waking. Why should not the dreamer himself who has the same ontological status as other persons in the dream be as unreal as they? (iii) I may dream about things happening to me over a week, a month or even a year, although the dream may last only a few minutes. How can the week, the month or the year be accommodated in the few minutes of the dream? As a matter of fact, I do not, and do not want to include the dream events in my life history. The entire dream world very strangely floats, hangs in the air, without any mooring in my life.[1]

Now even acknowledging the force of these arguments of Professor Kalidas Bhattacharya one may still wonder, how ever one can remember, or seem to remember, one's dream on waking. If the dreamer and the person remembering the dream are different persons, one unreal and the other real, then how is it possible to remember a dream? If the dream is not remembered by the subject on waking, it cannot even be rejected as unreal then. So the person dreaming and the person remembering the dream must be the same person. The difficulty is that if one dreams that one is a completely different person from the person who he is in waking consciousness, then how is the identification of these two persons possible? This shows that one can identify oneself with anyone one wants to, and with different persons at different times. It will not do to formulate a philosophical theory of the self only on the evidence of what we believe ourselves to be in the waking hours.

I shall begin my discussion of the emergence of the personal self by examining three theories of the no-person variety, of Hume, Nozick and Parfit, in that order.

HUME'S THEORY OF THE SELF

Hume in an oft quoted passage says:

> When I enter most intimately into what I call myself, I always stumble on some particular perception or other, of heat or cold, light or shade, love or hatred, pain or pleasure. I never can catch myself at any time without a perception and can never observe anything but the perception. . . . I may venture to affirm of the rest of mankind that they are nothing but a bundle or collection of different perceptions, which succeed each other with an inconceivable rapidity and are in perceptual flux and movement. The mind is a kind of theatre where several perceptions successively make their appearance, pass, repass, glide away, and mingle in an infinite variety of postures and situations. . . . The comparison of the theatre must not mislead us. They are the successive perceptions only, which constitute the mind. . . .[2]

Explaining Hume's theory, Bruce Anne says:

> The view Hume expresses here has come to be known as the Bundle Theory of the Self. Just as Bertrand Russell argued that physical things are bundles of qualities, Hume argued that even minds must be viewed as bundles. To say, on this view, that a quality exists in a mind is just to say that the quality belongs to some mind-bundle.[3]

There are various sorts of difficulties in Hume's theory. When he says 'when *I* enter most intimately into what I call myself' it is not clear what is that which enters most intimately into what I call myself and who is this I who call whatever it is myself. It is also not explained how a sequence of momentary ideas can be collected in a bundle. The metaphor of momentary perceptions which 'succeed another with inconceivable rapidity' is ~~of~~ falling rain-drops in a heavy shower. How can the falling rain-drops be collected together? Only when they fall on the ground that we can have a pool of water, where the rain water is collected, but *then* the drops are *not* successive. It is also not clear how I get my I-sense; is it also momentary, or is it of the series? If it is momentary, then at every moment there is a different I, as there is a different perception or idea. On the other hand, it cannot be momentary, for then memory, moral responsibility etc., cannot be explained. Yet according to Hume there cannot be identity of the person across time for the following reason.

Hume admits that there are gaps between the ideas or impressions succeeding each other; so the question is: What happens during these gaps between any two successive ideas? These gaps must be there, for the series of ideas and impressions, is a discrete series; to make a continuum of ideas and impressions their number has to be non-denumerable which is not possible. In any case, Hume himself admits that there are gaps between any two successive ideas. As there is just nothing in the gaps, there cannot be any personal identity.

Hume seems to be aware of this difficulty and tries to cover, and not solve it, by his theory that the 'different perceptions . . . succeed each other with an inconceivable rapidity', for there will be nothing during the gaps to experience then. The preceding perception cannot experience the gap, which is still to come, the succeeding perception cannot experience it as the gap has ceased to exist when it has come into being. This being the case there is no reason for Hume to hold on to the theory of inconceivable rapidity of succession; for even if the perceptions do not succeed each other with 'inconceivable rapidity' and the intervening gaps are lengthened, still the gaps will not be experienced as there will be nothing to experience them. The gaps are actually there, whether they are inconceivably short or very long, all incapable of being experienced; and if the existence of long gaps makes the unity of the self inconceivable, the inconceivably short gaps cannot solve this difficulty. To explain the immediately felt unity of the self it is necessary to deny the *existence* of gaps in consciousness, not merely their experience or conceivability.

This reveals another difficulty in Hume's theory. According to Hume ideas are associated by contiguity and similarity. But every idea is insulated from every other idea by a gap in consciousness on two sides between it and its preceding idea as well as its succeeding idea, it is not clear how there can be any association of ideas surrounded by gaps in consciousness. An idea will not be aware of what precedes it or succeeds it; it cannot be connected or associated with a preceding or a succeeding idea as all ideas are surrounded by gaps in consciousness; between two ideas there is just nothing. And it is not clear how this gap, although it is 'inconceivably' small, can be bridged. So there will be no contiguity.

It is only a *transcendent* observer or thinker who would be helped by the 'inconceivable rapidity' of succession of ideas into wrongly perceiving or conceiving an enduring self. The modern analogy of movie films may explain this point. The still photographs have to be projected on the screen with sufficient rapidity, and not inconceivable rapidity, to produce the illusion of continually moving objects to an observer who is *outside* the pictures. But in the case of perceptions succeeding one another with 'inconceivable rapidity' there is no transcendent subject who can have the illusion of an enduring self.

We may explain these difficulties in Hume's theory in some detail. Suppose 'a bundle of different perceptions' can be formed in some way. But then, either this bundle can be completed only when the person dies; till then the bundle will go on including almost infinite perceptions every day. Or, if the bundle is regarded as closed at any time, then the bundle the next day will be different, even if it includes all perceptions of the closed bundle. If bundles are regarded as collections or sets of perceptions, then we have an infinite series of ever wider sets of perceptions from birth till death of the person. Thus we have the almost infinite sequence of bundles:

$$B_1 \subset B_2 \subset B_{3\ldots\ldots} \subset B_{n\ldots\ldots}$$

The union of all the B_n's will be the same as the last bundle that one has at the time of death. Thus at every moment of waking life, one has a different self—it is almost the same as the Buddhist theory of momentary selves.

Now let us see how the so-called laws of association work. Suppose there is a perception P_1, and there is another perception P_2, which is either similar to P_1, or is contiguous in time. Now P_1 will *not* be associated with P_2 unless both P_1 and P_2 belong to the same bundle i.e., to the same self. If P_1 belongs to one self, and P_2 to another, then even if they are similar or contiguous in time, they will not be associated with each other. This shows that the so-called laws of association already *presuppose*, and hence, cannot explain, personal identity.

The most fundamental question which arises in this type of theory is that if none of the single perceptions is felt as myself how can a 'bundle of perceptions' amount to self-awareness? Is the origin of awareness of myself just bundling of perceptions, none of which is myself? How can a bundle give rise to an awareness of myself? The point is that the bundle of perceptions is possible only if the perceptions belong to the same person; that is, the bundle presupposes the actuality of the person whose perceptions are collected in the bundle.

NOZICK'S THEORY OF THE SELF

Robert Nozick in his *Philosophical Explanations* tries to develop the idea of the self from mental states. He finds the theory of a permanent self inadequate. Basing his argument on Shoemaker's assertion that self-awareness being 'immune to error through misidentification', Nozick states 'with a pre-existing I, however, there is always room for a mistake' (p. 90). So there cannot be any pre-existing I. 'The Vedānta theory is the *ātman* is *Brahman*. . . . . (Nozick's theory) does conflict with the view that this self exists independently of any act of synthesis, a contention massively and inconclusively debated between Vedāntists and Buddhists' (p. 94).

According to Nozick, the term 'I' is a linguistic device which is reflexively self-referring 'from the inside', 'with reflexive self-reference, it follows from—is part of—the sense the term necessarily self-refers in virtue of a feature bestowed in the token act of referring' (p. 76). 'From the fact that I have this property of being a self, it does not follow that the property is essential to my nature. Moreover, even though the capacity for reflexive self-reference is essential to being a self, and even though reflexive self-referring provides the access of a self to itself, it does not follow that it is of my essence (though actually I am a self) to be a self' (p. 79).

> Though it does not follow from considerations about how the term 'I' refers, it nonetheless is true, I think, that selves are essentially selves, that anything which is a self could not have existed yet been otherwise. I am an I—necessarily I am an I (p. 79).

To explain this point Nozick examines reflexive self-referring more closely. 'The token "I" refers to the entity (capable of self-referring) which produces the token. . . . Thus, within the reflexive self-referring act are components of action, intention, causal production' (p. 88).

> Let us imagine initially, acts without a doer, with no agent behind them. Better imagine acts so as to leave open the question of whether or not an agent is behind them. Acts A_1 . . . . . . A_n

> take place. These include (but are not restricted to) acts of applying the closest relation schema, unifying and synthesizing entities in classification, bringing together things to constitute demarcated entities (p. 88).

This synthesis which produces the self is momentary. Yet Nozick states '"If the self synthesizes itself at a time isn't it only a momentarily existing self? How then can we have identity over time?" The self synthesizes itself not only transversely, among things existing only at that time, but also longitudinally so as to include past entities including past selves which were synthesized' (p. 91).

Now Nozick distinguishes his theory of the self from Hume's theory. 'Doesn't the self-synthesizing view give the self the status of a collection or bundle (to use Hume's term) rather than a true unity?' (p. 94).

'What makes one mind one, rather than a composite of different entities?' (p. 95). The reply is: 'We can use the closest continuer theory of identity over time to specify how a whole may differ from the sum of its parts. . . . The closest continuer of a whole is not the sum of the closest continuers of the parts of the whole' (p. 99).

> Two notions have been intertwined in our discussion: first, that the identity of something can be maintained over time even though the parts change; second, the mere continued existence of all the parts is not enough to maintain the existence of the whole, presumably because the parts haven't remained (or entered) in certain relations to each other. Let us call the first a whole and the second a unity; something is a whole if its parts can be replaced, something is a unity if its parts must stay in certain relations for the entity to continue to exist. (p. 103)

The self is a unity, not a whole.

Now let us examine Nozick's theory. It has an advantage over Hume's theory of the self as a bundle of perceptions. Still, Nozick's theory involves many difficulties. Nozick accepts the doctrine of 'atomic-point-instants' (p. 46), i.e., he accepts the atomistic notion of time. He therefore, does not accept the possibility of anything enduring in time. He also does not accept the possibility of an extended thing. 'Since spatial and temporal distances involve some dissimilarity, any temporal or spatial breadth involves some sacrifice of (exact) similarity' (p. 46). Now if one accepts this theory that one thing can be strictly identical with itself only at one atomic-point-instant, then it is not clear how one can talk of 'acts $A_1 \ldots A_n$' taking place and how these acts can possibly include 'acts of applying the closest relation schema'. For, all the acts $A_1 \ldots A_n$ cannot take place simultaneously, they can only be successive, if there is no 'spatial breadth' in which they occur. But then it is not clear how they can be synthesized at one time; they are not all available at one time. They cannot leave their memory, for this would require an abiding self where the successive acts occur and then vanish leaving memory traces in the abiding self. Memory is not possible if acts 'take place' somewhere, and *that* somewhere is not available later to remember the acts. If there is no doer of the acts, then what acts, (acts 'taking place' even at different places?) are to be synthesized? All the acts to be synthesized must belong to one self. Otherwise, the act of synthesis will synthesize one act of one person with another act of another person and so on. When Nozick states 'Descartes can only reason "thinking is going on" and not "I think", thinking which is self-conscious is floating, not being tied to any "independently existing I". But then as all acts of thinking are self-conscious, and they are no one's thoughts, all thoughts will be synthesized, so that there is only one I.'

This difficulty of past acts vitiates also his solution to overcome the problem of momentary selves. It is not clear how the momentary self can 'include past entities including past selves which were synthesized' (p. 91). The past selves, like other past events, are dead and gone. They can be available only in memory. But memory already presupposes an enduring subject.

So Nozick's theory of synthesis of acts to generate a self is not satisfactory.

The very concept of 'closest continuer' (p. 33), requires an enduring transcendent observer. The very question whether *x* at time *t* is the same individual as *y* at later time t_2 requires a transcendent subject who knows *x* at *t*, and remembers it 'at a later time t_2'. Only someone who has known both, can raise the question whether they are identical. The spatial figures (Figures 14. 4–1. 6, p. 85) of dots are misleading for mental acts, which can never co-exist like dots on a paper.

There is another difficulty in Nozick's theory of synthesis. 'Thus within the reflexive self-referring act are components of action, intention, causal production' (p. 86). It is not clear whether feelings, emotions, beliefs, thoughts, etc. are components of the self-referring act. The different components like thinking, feeling, willing are not related to the self in the same way. But if the self be the synthesis of the components, then they are related in the same way to the synthesis. 'Acts $A_1 \ldots A_n$' 'include acts of applying the closest relation scheme unifying and synthesizing' (p. 88). Thus all the 'acts' are synthesized, 'brought together' 'to constitute demarcated entities'. This shows that only 'acts' are synthesized, there are no feelings, emotions which are not acts.

The main difficulty in Nozick's theory is that of explaining how one can obtain the 'acts' which are to be synthesized into the self. The point is that one can obtain these acts only by introspection; this means that the self is already presupposed in obtaining the so-called acts. One can introspect into one's own acts; it will not do to synthesize *any acts* to constitute the self.

PARFIT'S THEORY OF THE SELF

Derek Parfit in his *Reasons and Persons* has argued against theories of a permanent self. First of all he raises some problems of the identity of the self by thought experiments. He begins by describing an imaginary apparatus called 'Teletransporter'. 'When I press the button, I shall lose consciousness, and then wake up at what seems a moment later. In fact I shall have been unconscious for about an hour. The scanner here on earth will destroy my brain and body, while recording the exact states of all of my cells. It will then transmit the information by radio. Travelling at the speed of light, the message will take three minutes to reach the Replicator on Mars. This will then create, out of new matter, a brain and body exactly like mine. It will be in this body that I shall wake up. . . . Examining my new body, I find no change at all. Even the cut of my upper lip, from this morning's shave, is still there' (p. 201). Then Parfit imagines a branch-line case. 'The New Scanner does not destroy my brain and body. Besides gathering the information, it merely damages my heart. While I am in the cubicle, with green button pressed, nothing seems to happen. I walk out, and learn that in a few days I shall die. I later talk, by two-way television, to my Replica on Mars. Let us continue the story. Since my Replica knows that I am about to die, he tries to console me with the same thoughts with which I recently tried to console a dying friend. It is sad to learn, on the receiving end, how unconsoling these thoughts are. My Replica then assures me that he will take up my life where I leave off. He loves my wife, and together they will care for my children. And he will finish the book that I am writing. Beside having all of my drafts, he has all of my intentions. I must admit that he can finish my book as well as I could. All these facts console me a little. Dying when I know that I shall have a Replica is not quite as bad as simply dying' (p. 201).

We now examine Parfit's imaginary cases. Parfit distinguishes between qualitative and numerical identity. 'I' and 'my Replica' are qualitatively identical or exactly alike in body and mind. The question which Parfit poses is, whether on the strength of this qualitative identity, we are justified in postulating numerical identity so that there is only one person.

Now, it is not clear how the scanner and the replicator function. 'The Scanner here on Earth will destroy my brain and body, while recording the exact states of all my cells' (p. 199). If we take what Parfit says literally, then the scanner recording the exact states of all my cells will also record my consciousness of myself which is a feeling of total identity. Now the replicator on Mars 'will then create, out of new matter a brain and body exactly like mine' (ibid.). The replicator ought to produce a brain which has the awareness of being identical with myself. So in the branch-line case where there are two persons exactly alike in body and mind ought to have a consciousness of identity which is numerical. 'He loves my wife, and together they will care for my children. And he will finish the book that I am writing. Besides having all of my drafts, he has all of my intentions' (p. 201). 'It is strange that he has my love for my wife, he has all my intentions, yet he does not have the most basic feeling that I have about myself. There is no reason why he will not have the feeling of identity which I have with myself if the scanner does what it is said to do. If he has this feeling of identity with myself, then in spite of his being on Mars and my being on Earth would not stand in the way of his feeling that he is myseif.' 'In every other way, both physically and psychologically, my Replica is just like me. If he returned to Earth, everyone would think that he was me' (p. 200). It is immaterial if everyone thought that he was me; what would prevent my Replica from thinking that he was me?

The argument may be that if I am on Earth, then I cannot be on Mars at the same time. This is, indeed, objectively true; but this cannot prevent me from identifying myself with my replica. One *can* identify oneself with anything whatsoever. This point may be explained by a quotation from William James:

> The following vivid account of a fit of hasheesh-delirium has been given me by a friend: '. . . I next enjoyed a sort of metempsychosis. An animal or thing that I thought of could be made the being which held my mind. I thought of a fox, and instantly, I was transformed into that animal. I could distinctly feel myself a fox, could see my long ears and bushy tail, and by a sort of introversion felt that my complete anatomy was that of a fox, . . . I was next transformed into a bombshell, felt my size, weight, and thickness, and experienced the sensation of being shot up out of a giant mortar, looking down upon the earth, bursting and falling back in a shower of iron fragments'.[4]

The following points about this report may be noted:

(i) That the experience of this self-identification with anything that came to the mind was hallucinatory cannot detract from not merely its logical possibility, but also from the reality of the experience. It has now become fashionable in philosophy to examine imaginary cases to refute a philosophical theory of self-identity; there ought not to be any objection to using a hallucination, a vivid experience, for the same purpose. We shall, however, see that there are other more common types of experience of self-identification.

(ii) One may identify oneself with anything whatsoever; hence self-identification is radically different from personal identity for which either physical continuity, or memory or both are necessary. Robert Nozick's theory of closest continuer is as out of place here as the other theories of criteria of self-identity.

(iii) This is because here there is no question of knowing oneself as the same person over time. I may identify myself with a bombshell and when I do this I do not think if I remain the same person as the one who identified himself with a fox sometime ago. The point is that in self-identification there is no awareness of myself continuing over time. The question, of course, could be raised, but is not raised at all.

(iv) Identity as a relation is reflexive, symmetrical and transitive, consciousness is always directed to something, and to be directed to itself, it has to reflect on itself, to turn itself upon itself, to be related to itself. This is why self-consciousness involves a reflexive relation and Nozick formulates his theory of self-identity on the basis of a special kind of reflexive relation. In identifying myself with an object, say, a fox, I do not have to be reflexively aware of myself, although when I have identified myself with a fox, I know myself as a fox, *then* this reflexivity comes in. But the problem here is not how I know myself, but how I can possibly identify myself with a fox or whatever. Self identification is not symmetrical also, there is no question of the bombshell identifying itself with me when I identify myself with it. Nor is it transitive. *A* may identify himself with *B*, and *B* with *C*, but from this it does not follow that *A* identifies himself with *C*. This is because when *A* identifies himself with *B* he does this as he knows him. This is common in love; when *A* loves *B* it so often happens that he loves his own image of *B*.

(v) There is also a dis-identification which is presupposed in every act of self-identification. It is necessary to cease to identify myself with this person that I am now, in order that I may identify myself with the bombshell. There must be total forgetfulness of my previous identification. The exclusive concern with the experience of identification is not the same as the concern with the first person identity over time. This experience is not also a philosophical theory about what I am.

(vi) The difference between the usual problem of self-identity and self-identification becomes clear if we realize that in self-identification, the self that identifies itself with anything whatever, may be *ontologically* just the living body (behaviourism), or a self-substance (spiritualism), a momentary idea or perception (a self-less person); whatever *be* the self ontologically, it is the I-sense that is transferred from it to that with which the self identifies itself. The ontological self does not enter into this transference of I-sense. 'The third-person version' and 'the first-person version' do not differ in the same way as self-identity differs from self-identification; for even in the 'first-person over time and appropriate criteria, perhaps memory etc., will be relevant for explaining this identity and sense of identity. In the case of self-identification, only the experience of self-identification suffices, no other criteria are needed.

(vii) Yet we should note here that when I thus identify myself with anything, that thing does not remain that thing, but becomes 'ensouled'. When I feel myself a fox, the feeling is not the feeling which a fox has of itself; when I identify myself with a bombshell, I do not become an inanimate object, but import my feeling into it, ('felt my size. . . .' 'experienced the sensation of being shot up . . .' etc.).

Advaita Vedānta explains this type of phenomenon as a case of fusing or confusing of myself with any person or object. This confusion or fundamental unclarity about the real nature of my self is also a confusion about the nature of the object. This is the cause of emotional involvement with, or attachment to, a not-self. This attachment admits of degrees; in its initial stage the attachment expresses itself in the form of desire for a person or object. This desire makes us take pleasure in the thought of the desired object, wanting to *possess* it, i.e., have it *as mine.* When the attachment grows, the object, whether attained or not, is felt as mine, and at the most intense state, it is felt as *I.* We have a glimpse of this self-identification in empathy. But it is easier to identify oneself with the object of desire in dream. I may dream that I *am* a child, an old man, an angel, a giant or an animal. I may even dream that I am dead, but I retain consciousness and an awareness of my dead body. I do not dream that I am an inanimate object, a stick or a table. In a dream this identification is total, for then there is non memory of myself as I am in the waking state; if the memory persisted, it would have rankled and interfered with my identifying myself anew. That attachment admits of degrees is obvious; it is clear, for example, in the story of Tom Canty:

> By and by Tom's reading and dreaming about princely life wrought such a strong effect upon him that he began to act the prince, unconsciously . . . but at last his thoughts drifted away to far, romantic lands, and he fell asleep in the company of jeweled and gilded princelings who lived in vast palaces, and had servants salaaming before them or flying to execute their orders. And then, as usual, he dreamed that *he* was a princeling himself.[5]

Divided Minds

Parfit argues that our identity is not what matters. He imagines a case of a person who has two hemispheres of the brain with exactly the same abilities. Then he argues:

> Suppose that I am one of this minority, with two exactly similar hemispheres. And suppose that I have been equipped with some device that can block communication between my hemispheres. Since this device is connected to my eyebrows it is under my control. By raising an eyebrow I can divide my mind. In each half of my divided mind I can then, by lowering an eyebrow reunite my mind . . .
>
> When I disconnected my hemispheres, my stream of consciousness divided. But this division is not something that I experience. Each of my two streams of consciousness upto the moment of division. . .
>
> Consider my experience in my 'right-handed' stream. I remember deciding that I would use my right hand to do the longer calculation. This I now begin. In working at this calculation I can see, from the movements of my left hand that I am also working at the other. I might, in my right-handed stream, wonder how, in my left-handed stream, I am getting on. I could look and see. This would be just like looking to see how well my neighbour is doing at the next desk (pp. 246–47). My work is now over. I am about to reunite my mind.

Now let us examine this imaginary case. Before I divided my mind I may have decided 'to divide my mind for ten minutes, to work in each half of mind on one of the two calculations, and then to reunite my mind to write a fair copy of the best result' (pp. 246–47). But the difficulty is that I have two eyebrows. Is it necessary to lower both to reunite my mind? 'In each half of my divided mind I can then, by lowering an eyebrow, reunite my mind' (p. 246). Now, even if I remember in each half of my consciousness to lower the eyebrow over which the divided brain has control, it is not clear how the two eyebrows are lowered simultaneously. What my right-handed stream is doing with its eyebrow cannot be known by the left-handed stream. So, the possibility remains when the right-handed stream has lowered the left eyebrow, the left-handed stream continues to raise the right eyebrow. Even if I stand before a mirror, the left eye cannot see what the right eye sees. The right-handed stream and the left-handed stream are said to be like 'neighbours'. But it is not exactly like the relation of myself with my neighbour. I can see what my neighbour is doing. But it is difficult to see which eyebrow is raised or lowered in the case of a divided mind. Even if the two streams of consciousness could somehow act simultaneously in lowering both eyebrows, it will be fortuitous and cannot be planned. There is no explanation how ever the two streams, once divided, can ever become united.

THE ADVAITA VEDĀNTA THEORY OF DEEP SLEEP

According to Advaita Vedānta, in deep sleep the *antaḥkaraṇa* is withdrawn into its material cause which is *ajñāna* or *avidyā*. Because there is no *antaḥkaraṇa* in deep sleep, there cannot be any awareness of I, for, according to Advaita Vedānta, *ahaṁkāra* is a function of *antaḥkaraṇa*.

The question arises whether there is any *vṛtti* of *avidyā* in deep sleep. It has been argued by the author of *Vedānta-Paribhāṣā* that unless a *vṛtti* or *avidyā* becomes the object of deep sleep, or more accurately, the object of the witnessing consciousness, we cannot explain the memory of waking that I knew nothing then. That I knew nothing is not the same as I did not know anything; if I did not know anything, then I could not have said so, unless I knew that I did not know anything. To be able to say that I knew nothing, this knowing nothing must become an object of my knowledge.

According to Advaita Vedānta, every individual has three different bodies—the gross body, the subtle body and the causal body. The gross body consists of the anatomical and physiological parts; the subtle body consists of the *antaḥkaraṇa*, the ten sense-organs and motor organs, and the five *tanmātras*. The causal body is *avidyā* which is the cause of embodied existence of the individual. In the waking state there is awareness of these three bodies; in dream there is awareness of the gross body. In deep sleep there is awareness of only *ajñāna* which is the causal body, in which the other bodies are dissolved.

Arguments for the Advaita Vedānta Theory

In deep sleep there is no awareness of the ego. This shows that the ego and pure consciousness are different. This theory is very different from the Nyāya theory according to which it is the self which is the ego.[6] The argument that there is no awareness of the ego in deep sleep is manifold. First of all, there is the introspective evidence that there is no awareness of the ego at that stage. Against this argument that because there is no awareness of the ego therefore the ego itself is not present, cannot be accepted as valid. It may be that because there is no awareness of objects, the ego, even though present is not manifested. We become aware of our ego only when we have some awareness of objects, internal or external. There cannot be any awareness of ego pure and simple.[7]

This objection is not valid. It may be asked here whether there is no awareness at all during deep sleep or whether there is awareness but not related to objects. The first alternative is impossible, for consciousness or awareness is eternal; hence, even in deep sleep there cannot be total absence of consciousness. The second alternative also is not justified, for, relatedness with objects cannot be a condition of awareness of the self which is self-revealing.

Can we have memory of the ego during deep sleep? Even though there is no law that whatever is experienced is later remembered, still, if in deep sleep the self is aware of itself and if the ego were identical with the self, there will be consciousness of the ego during deep sleep. If on waking one remembers the self, then why should not one remember the ego?

The opponent may reply that the ego is the self and the awareness of the self cannot be destroyed, for the self is eternal and so also is its consciousness. Because the consciousness is eternal there cannot be any memory trace left by it. The psychological law is that we can remember an experience which we once had but do not have now. Experience and memory of the experience cannot co-exist. So, as self-consciousness is eternal, there cannot be any memory trace left by it. Hence, there is no memory of the ego during deep sleep even on waking.

The reply to this objection is that if there can be no memory of the ego experienced during deep sleep, then there cannot be any memory of yesterday's ego for the same reason. But according to Advaita Vedānta, the consciousness limited by the ego which one had yesterday is noneternal. Hence, there can be memory traces left by it and hence it can be an object of memory today and on subsequent days.

It may be objected that the ego during deep sleep may become an object of memory on waking from deep sleep for the person waking from deep sleep has a memory, 'I slept very comfortably'.

The reply is that the witnessing consciousness which is self-revealing and is the real nature of the self which is bliss is eternal. Although the self is always self-revealing, still during the two stages of waking and dreaming it is not clearly manifested because of the wrong belief that I am a man, I am a Brahmin etc. But during deep sleep, there is no distortion due to wrong beliefs, the witnessing consciousness reveals itself clearly. At that stage, though the *avidyā* covers or conceals the *Brahman,* still it cannot conceal the witnessing consciousness which reveals it. If the *avidyā* which conceals reality could not have been revealed by witnessing consciousness, then there would not have been any evidence for the existence of *avidyā.* Hence it is proved that in deep dreamless sleep, three things—bliss, self and positive *ajñāna* are experienced. On waking, these three experiences are remembered in the form, 'I had a pleasant sleep, I could not be aware of anything.'

It may be argued here that the three things, namely, bliss, the self and positive *ajñāna,* which are objects of experience cannot be experienced through any mode of the *antaḥkaraṇa* (the inner sense). For, during deep sleep there is no mode of *antaḥkaraṇa.* If it is said that these experiences are by the witnessing consciousness, then the problem arises that the witnessing consciousness being eternal, cannot leave any memory trace and so, cannot be remembered on waking. Yet it cannot be doubted that we do have such a memory on waking from deep sleep.

The reply to this objection is that even though in deep sleep there is no mode of the *antaḥkaraṇa,* still, *avidyā* which veils the consciousness during deep sleep assumes the three modes about bliss, the self and the veil. The different states of the apparent consciousness qualified by those modes reveal the self, bliss and the *ajñāna* and then cease to exist, so the memory traces due to the nonpermanent modes of *avidyā* produce memory on waking 'I slept well, did not know anything'.

Now the objection is that the self which experiences deep sleep and the self that remembers on waking are different selves. For the self which remembers on waking is the self qualified by the *antaḥkaraṇa.* Thus, the self which experiences is not identical with the self that remembers. This makes memory inexplicable.

The reply to this objection is that according to Advaita Vedānta, even in the waking state, the self qualified by *avidyā* is the subject that remembers. The question then arises, what function does the *antaḥkaraṇa* have in waking? The reply is that the memory which is a function of the consciousness qualified by *avidyā* still requires the *antaḥkaraṇa* to state the remembered objects in language. The *antaḥkaraṇa* therefore, is that which initiates use of language only but is not the subject that remembers.

According to Advaita Vedānta then, we can know by postulation (*arthāpatti*) that during deep sleep there is absence of suffering and absence of cognition of objects. But bliss, self and *ajñāna* are objects of memory on waking.

Now the question arises, what happens to the ego during deep sleep? The answer is that in deep sleep there is no awareness of the ego and hence there is no memory of the ego on waking. But then a further question arises that if on waking, I say 'I slept well', it involves the awareness of the ego. The answer is that during deep sleep the ego is withdrawn into its material cause and in waking hours it is again produced. The only function of the awareness of the ego is that it indicates the self as conducive to explicit linguistic usage by making the self an object of determinate cognition. For this reason the self is never said to have any internal state without the ego. When the self is indicated by the awareness of the ego, then that ego appears as identical with the self. The ego has no function other than explicitly manifesting the self. That is why the self is explicitly manifested only by the ego.

The material cause of the ego is the beginningless, inexpressible *avidyā*. The supreme law of *karma* which is located in *avidyā* is the *nimittakāraṇa* of the ego. The ego has two powers, the power of knowledge and the power of action. It is manifested by the witnessing consciousness only. The ego produces the awareness of one self being an agent and a patient. Even though during deep sleep the ego is withdrawn into its material cause which is *avidyā*, still life continues, for life is the active power and is different from the ego. If, however, life and ego are regarded as identical, then we shall have to hold that in deep sleep the ego minus life merges in its material cause.

THE ADVAITA VEDĀNTA THEORY OF THE EGO

According to Advaita Vedānta philosophers, the empirical subject is pure infinite consciousness illusorily cognized as finite. There are three different theories about how this unreal appearance is caused—(i) *avacchedavāda*, (ii) *ābhāsavāda* and (iii) *pratibimbavāda*.

(i) According to the first theory, the empirical subject, i.e., the *jīva*, is pure consciousness illusorily restricted by *antaḥkaraṇa*, which is constituted by *manas*, *buddhi*, *citta* and *ahaṃkāra* (the I-sense or the ego). When there is an awareness of doubt or vacillation, it is the function of *manas* as an element of the *antaḥkaraṇa* (the inner sense). When there is awareness of certainty it is the function of the element of *buddhi* in the inner sense. The I-sense which is present in every cognition in the form 'I cognize' is due to the element of *ahaṃkāra* (ego) of the inner sense. Recollection or memory is due to the element of *citta* in the inner sense. As a matter of fact, the inner sense is a unity which does not contain these four factors but which only functions in four different ways in an epistemological context. Because of this functional difference the one *antaḥkaraṇa* is called by four names.

Now according to the *antaḥkaraṇa*, this *antaḥkaraṇa* is different in different individuals and so the individuals also are different. This theory is usually explained by a metaphor. Space is one and infinite; yet it is restricted by things like rooms etc. In a room, space inside is restricted by its walls, yet this space so restricted is not really a part cut off from the infinite space, but is identical with the infinite space which is not effected by being bound by the four walls of the room. Yet one may say that rooms of different sizes enclose different portions of the infinite space; so also the different empirical subjects are really partial manifestations of the infinite consciousness. If we accept this theory, then we can easily distinguish between finite selves and the infinite pure consciousness and so can explain how a finite self can meditate on the infinite consciousness. For meditation or contemplation requires a difference between that which contemplates and that which is contemplated upon. The contemplator and the contemplated cannot be identical as that would identify the subject of the act with the object ~~which~~ would make the action impossible (*kartṛ karma bhāva*).

(ii) According to the second theory, finite selves are so many reflections of the one infinite pure consciousness in the different *antaḥkaraṇas*. This theory also is explained with the help of a metaphor of the sun reflected in different pots of water. The reflected pure consciousness is the empirical subject (*ābhāsa evaca*, *Brahma-sūtra* 2.3.50).

Now, the question arises whether the reflection and the reflected are one or different. According to Sureśvara, the *bimba* (the original object) and the *pratibimba* (the reflection) are different. The *pratibimba* is the shadow (*chāyā*) of *ābhāsa* of the *bimba*. But the shadow is not real, is *mithyā*. Hence the finite selves being *pratibimbas* i.e., shadows, cannot be real.

(iii) According to the third theory, the *bimba* and the *pratibimba* are not really different, their difference is the product of *ajñāna* and is, therefore, itself *mithyā*. The face reflected in a mirror and the face itself are not really two objects. According to Vidyāraṇya, if the *bimba* and the *pratibimba* are really different then there cannot be any relation of reflection between them. One object cannot be a reflection of an altogether different object. According to the *ābhāsavāda* explained above [in (ii)], it is only the reflection which is illusory.

But this theory cannot be accepted because if it were illusory then it would have been cancelled by a true cognition of the form 'this is not the face'; but this cognition never arises. Hence it cannot be said that the reflection of the face in the mirror is illusory. It is, of course, true that one realizes that there is no face in the mirror, but this realization cancels not the face itself, but the relation of the face with the reflection in the mirror. As a matter of fact, what one recognizes is that this face reflected in the mirror *is* my face, which shows that the *bimba* and the *pratibimbavāda*, the object and its reflection, are not different, that they are really one.

There are some Advaita Vedānta philosophers who try to conceive the reflection as a copy or imprint of the object. But this interpretation of the relation between the reflection and the object reflected cannot be accepted. For the imprint, say, of a seal on a wax is of the same size and shape as the object itself, yet the face reflected in a small mirror is smaller in size than the face itself. So the reflection cannot be regarded as an imprint of an object, as on wax.

According to others the face reflected in the mirror is not the face which is on the body of the person. The reflection is a different face. But this theory too, cannot be accepted. If the face in the mirror is a different face, the question then inevitably arises: Where from does it come? What produces it? There cannot be any satisfactory reply to such questions. Moreover, everyone recognizes that his face which is on his body is reflected in the mirror, which shows that they are identical.

Against this theory it may be objected that if the face on the body and the face reflected in the mirror are one and the same, then how is it that the reflection is seen in the mirror? The reply to this objection is that the face seen as reflected in the mirror is the function of *ajñāna*. This *ajñāna* wrongly reveals one object as another, one object located here as the object located there and so on. When the face on the body is mistakenly cognized being in the mirror, this wrong cognition is the reflection.

According to some philosophers, there is no such thing as reflection. That we seem to see the reflection of our face in the mirror is an illusion. When we look at the mirror the light rays are reflected back on our face and therefore the eyes see the face itself. Unless the light rays are reflected back on to our face we cannot see our face. This reflection of the light rays requires the presence of a mirror and that is why we cannot see our face except in the presence of a mirror. Hence it is an illusion to see the reflection of the face in the mirror. Against this theory it is pointed out that what we see in the mirror cannot be the real face because in the mirror the image is inverted. If what we see in the mirror is the real face, then this inversion of the image becomes inexplicable. Hence it has to be admitted that the face and its reflection have different locations, and this difference in location can easily explain the inversion of the image.

We can easily explain how pure infinite consciousness can be the indwelling spirit of the *jīva*. This cannot be explained in *avacchedavāda*.

CONCLUSION

We have seen that there are two forms of the problems of the emergence of the self. One is to explain how a permanent self can emerge from fleeting, successive mental states or acts. According to Hume, my awareness of my self as an enduring centre of consciousness is really an illusion. But Hume fails to explain how the illusion arises. He uses the method of introspection in order to establish that there is no permanent self. Yet introspection itself is impossible if an enduring self is not already presupposed. A momentary idea cannot introspect itself for it is not yet felt as I. Nozick, too, starts with acts which are to be synthesized into a permanent self. But the acts which are to be synthesized cannot be acts floating in the air. Nozick does not state that these acts are to be obtained from introspection. But neither does he explain how one can get these acts which are then synthesized into a permanent self. The Buddhist school of Vijñānavāda seems to offer the best theory of this type. According to Vijñānavāda, each momentary state knows itself as I, so that we have a succession of I's—I_1, I_2, I_3 . . . The difference between this Buddhistic theory and those of Hume and Nozick is that while according to this school of Buddhism each mental state itself is an I, according to Hume and Nozick, no single perception or act is an I. Hence the problem both in Hume and Nozick is to explain the source of the elements which are to be synthesized into a permanent self. Both according to Hume and Yogācāra Buddhism, the belief in an enduring self is a wrong belief, while according to Nozick this is a construction which is not necessarily unreal. According to Yogācāra Buddhism, the succession of momentary I's is mistaken for an enduring self and there is no mystery here except a confusion due to nescience; I_1 mistakes itself as identical with I_2 and so on. When this original nescience is removed, the succession of I's stops and there is nothing thereafter. This is the traditional Indian interpretation of *nirvāna.*

The problem of Advaita Vedānta is very different. The reality is not a succession of momentary mental states or acts but is universal impersonal consciousness. Consciousness cannot be mine or yours, for consciousness is the ultimate owner of the body-mind complex, but there is no owner of consciousness. The problem here is to explain our common experience of ourselves as persons. This is, of course, a wrong belief which is removed by knowledge of the real nature of consciousness. But this wrong belief which is nescience is beginningless. We do not begin with an awareness of impersonal consciousness and then somehow acquire consciousness of ourselves as persons. Thus the Advaita theory of emergence of the self is neither a historical process nor a logical construction.

NOTES AND REFERENCES

1. *Mandukyopaniṣader Katha*, p. 8.
2. *A Treatise of Human Nature*, edited by L.A. Selby-Bigge, Oxford, 1988, Bk 1, Pt. 4, see 6, pp. 252–53.
3. *Metaphysics*, Basil Blackwell, 1986, p. 167.
4. William James, *The Principles of Psychology*, Vol. II, pp. 121–22.
5. Samuel L. Clemens, *The Prince and the Pauper*, Masterpiece Library, Magnum Books, New York, 1968, p. 18.
6. *Ahaṃkarasyasrayo yam mano matrasya gocarah, Bhāṣāparicchedah* Verse.
7. *Atha susuptau visayanubhavabhavat satopyahanikarasy navabhasah—Vivaran-aprameya Saṁgrahah*, p. 75.

3

Process of Existence and Psycho-Social Culture

MAHESH TIWARY

The present essay is intended to present an analytic description of the concept of philosophy and culture based on the material available in canonical (*piṭaka*), non-canonical (*anu-piṭaka*), commentarial (*aṭṭhakathā*), and ancillary (*pakiṇṇaka*) texts in Pāli. The concept of science may be taken up separately in Part IV. In doing so, an attempt is being made to narrate something as evinced mainly from the discourses of the Buddha and commented upon by some of the saint-scholars in the tradition. The conventional time-passage is 600 BC when the Buddha was on his righteous way-faring (*cārikā*) for forty-five years, giving discourses to all, without any discrimination. His such discourses are the basic materials for the present essay.

The term *philosophy* is generally used for *darśana*. The term *darśana* does not occur in Pāli canonical texts in the above sense. The equivalent term, which may be located, is the *dhamma*. The Buddha always used the expression—'I preach the *dhamma*'—'*Dhammaṃ O, Bhikkhave, desmi*'. In the context, taking *dhamma* for philosophy, it may be said that 'the Buddhist philosophy is a system of *psycho-ethical thought* as well as a *practical way of virtuous life*. The two proceed together as the two wheels of a chariot to bring a harmonious and balanced state of life, here and hereafter as relishable Truth. The former prescribes a number of principles like—Law of Dependent Origination (*paṭiccasamup-pāda*), four Noble Truths (*catu-sacca*), three-fold nature of Reality (*tilakkhaṇa*), law of *kamma* (*kamma-vipāka-vidhi*) moving towards realization of a state of eternal Bliss (*nibbāna*) etc. and the latter goes for categorical indication of a path having three steps for realization of the principles (*pariyatti*) as a fact (*paṭipatti*) in this state of existence. The *dhamma* signifies neither any type of imaginative flight nor a state of psychic bewilderness but refers to a raft rightly moving with beings from this *shore* to that *shore.* In this way, it is a system of practical realization within and without in ascending order.

Due to the limited scope of the present essay, it is very difficult to say even a few words about the major ideals or practices, so beautifully adumberated with a vast treasure of materials but it would be wise to remain restrained with one of them inter-linked for the purpose. In the situation, *history* comes to help to say something about one, which is historically the *one,* in transmission. And what is that?

It is evident from the text that the Buddha, immediately after getting enlightenment under the *Bodhi* Tree, pondered over the doctrine known as *paṭiccasammupāda* or the Law of Dependent Origination in *anuloma* and *paṭilomanaya* and as such, this stands as the first natural flow of expression of his realization. This being the first historical expression, a humble attempt is being made to say a few words about it under the caption *Process of Existence.* Again, it has a definite purpose for its fruitful materialization and as such it requires a brief exposition on psychic training. The combined effect of the two is the saturation of the same through the practical life of the beings. It has been briefly presented here as psycho-social culture. As its background, the essay has three main parts, namely, process of existence, psychic culture and social culture.

PROCESS OF EXISTENCE

The mystery before man has been the mystery of man itself. When did he come into existence, how did the process of life begin, how has the unbroken way-faring been accelerated, and how long it will go on revolving are the several questions which have been generating the ripples of inquisitiveness on the awakened as well as the dormant surface of mind of the seers from the hoary past. There is a historical tradition of sincere and serious efforts of penetrating into the core of the mystery and unearthing the reality as a basic fact. This ushered forth tremendous development of variegated thought-processes together with cross-currents in different systems of Indian philosophy. There is also the story of an Indian saint who endeavoured incessantly for thousands of existences in search of the mystery and lastly reached the stage of attainment of the fortunate moment of relishing the flavour of soothing experience of realization and visualization of the truth face to face. He could not check himself but due to prevailing ecstatic joy came out through vocal expression—

Gahakāraka diṭṭhosi, puna gehaṃ na kāhasi,
Sabbā te phāsukā bhaggā, gehakuṭaṃ visaṅkhitaṃ,
Visaṅkhāragattaṅ cittaṃ, taṇhāṇaṃ khayamajjhagā.[1]

O House-builder, you have been seen, you will not build the house furthermore. All your rafters have been broken, the ridge-pole has been dismantled, the consciousness has attained a state of non-accumulation, there is the total negation of attachment.

The saint is none else than the Buddha. The revelation is the unearthing of the mystery of the process of existence on the spiritually highlighted spot of *bodhimaṇḍa* amidst the rhythmic resoundings of awakening generated by the wisdom-inspired wavelets of River *nirajjarā* within and without.

Then what is the process of existence? The answer is that—'it is the name of the continuous revolving of the five aggregates, twelve bases and eighteen elements'. The three expressions—aggregates (*khaṇda*), bases (*āyatana*), and elements (*dhātu*) are the simple indication of the 'physio-psycho amalgam' which constitutes the personality of a man. The man comes into being, dies, renews again the form of becoming, meets disintegration and goes on maintaining the unbroken series of repeated existence. This unbroken continuity of appearance and disapperance of a man is the *saṁsāra,* which we name in the present context as the process of existence. The ancients say:-

Khandhānaṃ ca paṭipāṭi, dhātu-āyatanānaṃ ca,
Abbocchinnaṃ vattamānā, saṃsāro ti pavuccati.[2]

Then why does a man go on renewing himself in this process of becoming? The answer as available is very simple. He has a companion, of course, not knowingly and because of having association with such a one, he falls under its blinding influence which by its nature makes him do so. It is the *taṇhā,* the attachment towards worldlings. It functions broadly in three ways in generating the urge for relishing the sensual pleasure (*kāma-taṇhā*), delightful craving for maintaining and feeling one's own individuality (*bhava-taṇhā*), and the strong sense of hatred and antipathy towards others in general and their prosperity in particular (*vibhāva-taṇhā*).[3] Its multiplicity with respect to variegated forms of objects weaves the snare of irrational longings and develops into the thickets of likes and dislikes like the ever-increasing flames amidst consumables for the present state of existence as well as the states to come. Thus attachment towards the worldlings is the engendering force in making the wheel of becoming revolve and putting the beings in the whirlpool of suffering. The Buddha has rightly observed:-

Taṇhā dutiyo puriso, dīgha-addhāna-saṃsāraṃ,
Etthabhāvaṃ-aññāthābhāvo, saṃsāraṃ nātivattai.[4]

The man with *attachment* as companion, the second one, has been passing through the passages of repeated existence, appearing and disappearing and finding no escape therefrom.

Then what is the process of the process of existence? The answer to this question is the most valuable contribution of the Buddha. For explaining this process, he has introduced a *law* which has been named as the Law of Dependent Origination or the *paticcasam-mupāda.* This law is the theme of the Buddha's *dhamma* and answer to so many philosophical problems along with the present one. The Buddha contemplated upon this law in direct and indirect way immediately after his enlightenment and examined its validity at the intellectual and experiential levels. It is after such realization that he made the lion roar—'thus is the way of the arising of suffering and this the way of cessation of suffering'. His such resounding is seen under the Bodhi Tree as—*Evametassa Kevalassa dukkhakkhandhassa samudayo hoti. . . Evametasa kevalassa dukkhakkhandhassa nirodho hoti.*[5]

The Law of Dependent Origination explains that there is nothing like a self-independent entity. Everything comes into being depending on the other. When one exists, there is the possibility of existence of the other; when one does not exist, the possibility of existence of the other is also not seen. In the background, there are twelve links which make the wheel of becoming revolve. They exist depending upon each other. The twelve links are:-

1. ignorance (*avijjā*),
2. activities (*saṅkhāra*),
3. birth consciousness (*viññāṇa*),
4. mind and body (*nāma-rūpa*),
5. six senses (*saḷāyatana*),

6. touch *(phassa)*,
7. feeling (*vedanā*),
8. desire *(taṇhā)*,
9. craving *(upādāna)*,
10. becoming *(bhava)*,
11. birth (*jati*) and
12. decay and death (*jarā-maraṇa*).[6]

With these links the three circles of existence have been illustrated. The first two links—'ignorance' and 'activities' belong to the past. The last two links 'birth' and 'decay' and 'death' belong to the future. The remaining eight links in the middle belong to the present state of life. It has been shown that depending on the past life, there is the existence of the present one and depending on the present one, there is the possibility of future life. It is in this way that the circle of existence goes on revolving and exhibits the *saṃsāra* as a fact of life. It proceeds as—'depending on the ignorance, there arise activities; depending on the activities, there arises birth-consciousness; depending on the birth-consciousness, there arise mind and body; depending on mind and body, arise the six senses; depending on the six senses, there arises touch; depending on the touch, there arises feeling; depending on the feeling, there arises desire, depending on the desire, there arises craving; depending on the craving, there arises becoming; depending on becoming, there arises birth; depending on birth, there arise decay and death. The process of existence continues in this way. It may be seen that all the twelve links are interlinked with one another. Being united to exist in this way, one comes into being depending on the other. The process of becoming in this way is called '*anuloma—paticcasamuppādanaya*'. So long the twelve links are united, there is the possibility of continuity of revolving of the wheel of becoming (*bhavacakka*). When any one of them is broken, the others are naturally broken and the process of becoming comes to a stop. This has been explained in the '*patiloma-paṭicca-samuppādanaya*'.

It is further said that—'with the cessation of ignorance, there is the cessation of the activities; with cessation of the activities, the birth consciousness ceases to be; with the cessation of the birth consciousness, mind and matter do not arise; with the cessation of the arising of mind and matter, there does not arise the touch; when the touch ceases to exist, there is not the arising of feeling;

with the cessation of feeling, the desire does not arise, when there is no arousal of desire, craving does not come to function; with the stopping of the functioning of the craving, there is no further becoming; when there is no becoming, there is no birth. After the cessation of birth, the decay etc. come to a stop. It is in this process that the revolving of the wheel of becoming reaches an end. This Law of Dependent Origination through its direct way of functioning explains the way of continuity of the chain of repeated existence and through its indirect way exhibits the possibility of its cessation.

What then is the nature of the twelve links? A brief description is appended here to introduce each one of them.

(1) *Ignorance (avijjā)*: For easy communication, the term *avijjā* is generally rendered as ignorance. But it has a definite meaning. Really speaking, that which covers the nature of reality generates psychic darkness, bewilders the consciousness and does not allow one to visualize that truth is ignorance (*dhammasabhāva-paṭicchādanalakkhanā avijjā*). It is a psycho-ethical phenomenon. Under its blinding influence, the 'suffering (*dukkha*), causes of suffering (*dukkha-samudayo*), cessation of suffering (*dukkha-nirodha*), the path leading to the cessation of suffering (*dukkhanirodhagamini paṭipadā*), the existence in the past (*pubbanta*), existence in future (*aparanta*), the state of existence in the present (*pubbantāparanta*), and the Law of Dependent Origination (*ida-paccayatā*) are not understood.

One takes the worldlings as a permanent source of joy and clings to them. The truth appears as untrue and untruth as true.

(2) *Activities* (*saṅkhāra*): The *saṅkhāra* is a multi-significance term. It has a number of senses in different contexts. Here it refers to the three-fold activities, namely physical, vocal and mental. It should be remembered that the activities are basically mental. They are named physical and vocal because of appearance through different doors. Thus the moral and immoral activities of *kāmāvacara*-sphere, *rūpāvacara*-sphere and *arūpāvacara*-sphere are referred to by the term (*saṅkhāra*). From the standpoint of consciousness, it is the name of twenty-nine types of consciousness, namely, twelve types of *kāmāvacara* immoral consciousness, eight types of *kāmāvacara* moral consciousness, five of *rūpāvacara* moral consciousness and four types of *arūpāvacara* moral consciousness.[7] From the standpoint of their manifestation through doors, it may be said that the three types of

physical immoral activities like killing, stealing and indulging in sexual misdeeds, the four types of vocal immoral activities like speaking untruth, slandering, using harsh speech and taking delight in useless talk; and three types of mental immoral activities as greed, hatred and wrong views are the ten types of immoral activities. Refraining from them are the ten types of moral ones. These twenty types of activities belong to *kāmāvacara*-sphere. The five types of activities of *rūpāvacara*-sphere and the four types of that of the *arūpāvacara*-sphere are mental and ecstatic in nature. All these activities are generated by ignorance and therefore it is stated as—*avijjā paccayā saṅkhāra.*

(3) *Birth-Consciousness* (*viññāna*): The literal meaning of the term *viññāna* is consciousness. In technical sense, it refers to a type of consciousness which connects one form of existence with the others. It means a type of resultant consciousness which functions as taking a being from one state of existence to another. What it may be? It is one of the nineteen types of resultant consciousness. Here it should be understood that a consciousness arises, ceases and yields its similar resultant on mind. The way of yielding resultant moral and immoral consciousness is not the same because of the fact that diverse nature of roots are associated with them. All the twelve types of immoral consciousness yield only one type of resultant which is of the nature of making the mind dull as—*upekkhā-sahagata-santīraṇa-akusala-vipāka.* Sometimes, the eight types of moral consciousness function with weak volition. Because of their being so, they also produce only one type of resultant that is the dullness of mind with moral orientation. It is technically named—*upekkhā-sahagata-santīraṇa-kusala-vipāka.* The eight types of moral consciousness of *kāmāvacara*-sphere yield eight types of similar resultants. Similarly, the five types of moral consciousness of *rūpāvacara*-sphere and the four types of moral consciousness of *arūpāvacara*–sphere yield five types and four types of resultants respectively. Thus the twenty-nine types of immoral and moral consciousness of three spheres yield nineteen types of resultants.[8] These resultants are capable of uniting a being from one state of existence to another and in this sense they are collectively called *viññāna.* What arises is thus the arising of the birth-consciousness. Since they are the resultants of the moral and immoral types of consciousness, they naturally arise depending on them. Therefore, it is called—*saṅkhāra-paccayā-viññṇaṃ.* Here it may be understood that the *viññāṇa* being the resultant consciousness

is a passive state having potentiality of generation of activities just like a seed. It is, in the true sense, understood as a *kammabīja.*

(4) *Mind and Matter* (*nāma-rūpa*) : *Nāma* stands for mind. It is the name of the subtle *dhammas,* both consciousness and psychic factors. It refers to the four mental aggregates, namely, feeling aggregate (*vedanā-khandha*), knowing aggregate (*saññā-khandha*), mental disposition aggregate (*saṅkhāra-khandha*) and consciousness aggregate (*viññāṇa-khandha*). The first three include the fifty-two types of psychic factors and the fourth one indicates the one hundred and twenty-one types of consciousness. Both the psychic factors and the consciousness are in the sprouting stage. They appear as a complex unit capable to step towards functioning to think. It is the initial form of the functional consciousness.

The word *rūpa* refers to the four types of basic material qualities (*bhūta-rūpa*) and twenty-four types of generated material qualities (*upādā-rūpa*), altogether twenty-eight in number. In the present context, *hadaya-vatthu* or the seat of consciousness is understood. It is said that due to the force of the *kamma,* both the mind (*nāma*) and matter (*hadaya-vatthu*) appear simultaneously after the arising of the birth-consciousness.

(5) *Six sense-bases* (*saḷāyatana*) : Eye (*cakkhu*), ear (*sota*), nose (*ghāna*), tongue (*jivhā*), body (*kāya*) and mind (*mana*) are the six sense-bases. Each of the six sense-bases is in the form of an energy that performs a definite type of action. The eye may not be understood as the eye-ball or the external form of the eye, visible and manifested. It, in its real sense, is the energy to see (*dassana-samatthatā*). Similarly, the ear refers to an energy to hear (*savana-samatthatā*), nose as an energy to smell (*ghāyana-samatthatā*), tongue as an energy to relish (*sāyana-samatthatā*) and the body as an energy to touch (*phusana-samatthatā*). Mind is an energy to think. The first five bases are material and the last one is mental. They arise depending on mind and matter and hence are stated as—*nāma-rūpa-paccayā saḷyāyataṇaṃ.*

(6) *Touch* (*phassa*) : Energy is the flow of action. As soon as the six sense-bases come into being, their functions with reference to objects begins. There are six kinds of objects, namely, visible object (*rūpa*), audible object (*sadda*), odorous object (*gandha*), sapid object (*rasa*), tangible object (*phoṭabba*) and ideational object (*dhamma*). Each sense-base has a definite object and it appears in its range according to situation. On appearance of an object in the

range of a sense-base, there is the initial contact of the two. It is called *phassa*. Since there are six sense-bases and six corresponding objects, there are six types of touches; such as touch with the eye-base and the visible object, the ear-base and the audible object and so on. These touches originate on the bases or rather the sense-bases and therefore, it is said—s*alyatanapaccayā phasso.*

(7) *Feeling* (*vedanā*) : A touch of an object with a sense-base results in the generation of feeling. *Vedanā* is the name of an innocent reaction of the mind towards the object. In generic parlance, it is the experience. In specific sense, it is the attitude of mind of receiving the object in aggreeable, or disagreeable or indifferent manner. In this way, there are three types of feelings, namely, pleasant feeling (*sukhā-vedanā*), unpleasant feeling (*dukkhā-vedanā*) and indifferent feeling (*upekkhā-vedanā*). Again, the pleasant feeling expresses itself as physical (*sukhā-vedanā*) and mental (*somanassa-vedanā*). Similar are the expressions of unpleasant feelings like physical unpleasant feeling (*dukhā-vedanā*) and mental unpleasant feeling (*somanassa-vedanā*). Such classifications make the feelings five in number. It is said in this context that the indifferent feeling can only find expression through the mind. Such an experience of neither feeling pain nor pleasure can only be experienced at the mental level. However, the Suttantika tradition includes 'indifference' (*upekkhā*) as physical too. Further analysis of feeling is seen from different standpoints and the number increases upto one hundred and eight. All these varieties of feelings arise depending on the 'touch', and therefore, the text as usual proceeds as—*phassa-paccaya avedanā.*

(8) *Desire* (*taṇhā*): Ignorance is at the root and as such generates a bewildered state of psychic darkness in viewing things. The things which are subject to suffering, are also subject to happiness. The sensual pleasure which is like a heap of blazing fire, appears as a source of joy. It inspires thirst for worldlings and gives rise to a leaning to have them. We name it 'desire' (*taṇhā*).

The worldlings as stated earlier are broadly classified into six objects. The desire also manifests with respect of these six types of objects. They may be the desire for visible object (*rūpa-taṇhā*), audible object (*sadda-taṇhā*), odorous object (*gaṇdha-taṇhā*), sapid object (*rasa-taṇhā*), tangible object (*phoṭabba-taṇhā*) and ideational object (*dhamma-taṇhā*). Further, on the basis of the varieties of the objects, they increase the varieties of desire. They all arise depending on 'feeling', therefore, it is said that—*vedanā-paccayā taṇhā.*

(9) *Craving* (*upādāna*): *Upādāna* may be understood with reference to *taṇhā.* A simple desire to have something is *taṇhā*; a strong desire for the same is *upādāna.* A desire to have a thing which is not achieved is *taṇhā,* just like stretching the hands in the darkness by thieves. Taking of things which belong to someone else forcefully is *upādāna,* just like taking other's belongings by the thieves. The former is the opposite to a state of less desire, the latter is to that of satisfaction. Harsh speech, scolding, cursing, beating etc., are examples of craving (*upādāna*). The latter (*upādāna*) comes into being depending on the former (*taṇhā*), therefore, the description proceeds as—*taṇhā paccayā upādānaṃ.*

(10) *Bhava* (*becoming*): The literal meaning of the term *bhava* is a state of becoming. It is generally used in two senses, namely *kamma-bhava* and *upapatti-bhava.* The former refers to the state of activities, the latter to that of coming into being. In the present context, the former is applicable. It is another name of *saṅkhāras* which means twenty-nine types of consciousness as cited before. The craving generates a strong urge to have the desired thing. For aquisition of the same, the moral and immoral activities again start. Here one may argue that why are the supramundane activities not counted in the present context. The reason is obvious, for the supramundane activities are the eliminating *dhammas.* They gradually eliminate the previous accumulations and make the consciousness free from them. It is for this reason that none of the supramundane activities are included in way of making categorical statements of the activities related to becoming. The *bhava* appears depending on *upādāna* and in explaining the sequence it is stated as—*upādāna-paccayā bhavo.*

(11) *Birth* (*jati*): Here birth means the unification of the previous state of existence with the present one. It takes place in the womb of the mother in the moment of *paṭsandhi.* In the real sense it is the arising of any one of the nineteen types of resultant consciousness as a *kammabīja* having the potentiality to sprout forth. It is the state of the coming into being of life. It takes place depending on the *bhava* and therefore, the text in its usual way states—*bhava-paccayā jati.*

(12) *Decay* and *Death* (*jarāmaraṇa*): The term *jarā* (decay) is the leaning of the being towards destruction in the flow of impermanence. It may be understood that there are two expressions of it, namely *khaṇika-jarā* and *pākaṭa-jarā.* The former is the name of mo-

mentary decay. Every moment the being in existence moves towards it. In the fluxional nature of reality, there are arisings and ceasings in every moment. It starts from the second moment of existence and continues till the arising of the *cuti-citta*.

The latter is the name of apparently visible decay. When the body is broken, it becomes weak and pale, bones become visible through the thin layers of skin, wrinkles appear on the face, hair become grey, we with a sense of grief say, 'old age has come'. Here both the forms of decay are meant as *jarā*.

Maraṇa means the destruction of the present state of existence. It is the arrival of death-consciousness (*cuti-citta*) and disconnection of the present flow of life. It is the basic fact connected with life and cannot be ignored. The present state of existence comes to an end with it. This end is not the final one but is renewed again and the process revolving like a wheel goes on continuing.[9]

This simple description of the above twelve links may reveal the fact that each link is dependent on the other. When the former exists, there is the possibility of arising of the other. Existing interdependently, they maintain the process of existence. Here an attempt is being made by the later *ācariyas* to make the functioning of the law clear. They are of the opinion that while explaining the *avijjā* and *saṅkhāra* arising depending upon each other, the *taṇhā, upādāna* and *bhava* should also be included. Then the order may be *avijjā, taṇhā, upādāna, saṅkhāra* and *bhava*. It will form the first unit of five modes (*ākāra*). The second unit, in this way, will be the *viññāṇa, nāma-rūpa, saḷāyatana, phassa* and *vedanā*. While exhibiting *taṇhā, upādāna,* and *bhava* as interdependent *dhammas*, the *avijjā* should be prefixed and the *saṅkhāra* should come just before *bhava*. It will take the form as *avijjā, taṇhā, upādāna, saṅkhāra,* and *bhava*. It will be the third unit. The last two links *jāti* and *jarāmaraṇa* should be understood as *viññāṇa, nāma-rūpa, saḷāyatana, phassa* and *vedanā*. It will be the fourth unit. Thus they go on to make the twenty modes.[10]

The twelve links being extended into four units of five links each make twenty modes. It provides an intellectual exercise to display the fact in the way that the first unit of five serves as the cause (*hetu*) in the past to generate the second unit of five as effect in the present. The third unit of five in the present serves as the cause for generation of the last unit of five as effect in the future.[11]

The four units of five meet on three junctions in the process of their functioning. The first unit meets with the second one, the second with the third and the third with the fourth. These three meetings are called the three junctions (*sandhi*) in the process.

From the standpoint of time-period, the three consecutive forms of existences; the past, the present and the future, have been taken into consideration. Depending on the past existence, there comes into being the present form of existence and similarly, depending on the present one, there will be the coming up of the future form of existence. The *avijjā* and *saṅkhāra*, the two links, refer to the past form of existence. The remaining eight links between the two indicate the present state of existence. The *jarā* and *maraṇa* represent the future state of existence. These three forms of existence are the three periods, technically called, *addha*.

Marking the continuity of the process of existence, a natural inquisitiveness leans towards knowing the root cause of the process. It is clear that the twelve links or the twenty modes are responsible for making the wheel of becoming revolve. But what are the main forces or the force working behind that? Going deep into the nature of each link and making a critical examination of their functioning, it becomes evident that *avijja* and *taṇhā* are the main forces working individually as well as collectively. Therefore, they are called the two roots (*mūla*). They are the accelerating forces behind the process of existence.

Now, coming to this point there is again an inquisitiveness about the beginning of the process of existence. On this issue the Buddha is very clear that 'the *saṃsāra* is beginningless, its starting point is not known. One cannot say that it started during the time of such and such Buddha or during the reign of such and such king and it was not existing before that—*anamataggo, bhikkhave, ayam samsāro, purimā koṭi assa na paññāyati*'.[12] Moreover, he does not find any utility in knowing that. His attitude is more clear from the simile of the man sought with an arrow and making bewildered statement.[13]

Then how long will it continue? The question is simple but the answer is very difficult. No categorical statement seems plausible in this regard. But there is the possibility of its cessation, as a fact, by making a *dhammika*-way-faring, through the practice and experience in gradual purification steps—*sīla, samadhi* and *paññā* and culminating in realization and face to face visualization of the ultimate goal of life, *nibbāna*.[14]

PSYCHIC CULTURE

The practical aspect of Buddhist philosophy is the prescription of a *path,* specially expressed with terms like—*magga* and *patipadā,* denoting the senses—'exerting continuously' and generating purity at each step respectively. It has three gradual steps, namely; *sīla, samādhi,* and *paññā.*

Sīla exercises restraints over physic and speech-doors and regulates the activities of man in a way to disassociate from the three immoral roots, namely; *lobha* (greed), *dosa* (hatred) and *moha* (ignorance). The physical and vocal misdeeds, in the process, are curtailed. It is called *physico-vocal culture.*

Samādhi has its role at the mind door in not allowing the immoral forces to harbour which have not so far arisen; eliminating those which are already at work and putting a check on the wandering of consciousness. It, in due course, minimizes the mental misdeeds and inspires the three moral roots—*alobha* (sacrifice), *adosa* (friendliness) and *amoha* (right view) to function fearlessly. It gradually generates a state of purity within. We name it *psychic culture.*

Paññā removes the darkness of ignorance, generates the light of wisdom, makes the three-fold nature of *reality* crystal clear and moving forward, inspires one to relish the flavour of the *path* (*magga*) and *fruit (phala)* of *sainthood.* It is, in this way, named as *intuitional culture.*

The three, of course, function at three units of specific doors, have both the individual and collective efforts internally combined in ushering forth the generation of purification of consciousness. The reason is obvious that 'the beings are purified because of the purification of consciousness, resulting in the emergence of inseparable unification of happiness, like the ever-accompanying of the shadow of a man:

'citta-pariyodānā sattā parisujjhanti'.

'Tato naṃ sukhamanveti,
chāyā va anapāyinī'.

The present essay is devoted to briefly introducing the second step of the path in the name of *psychic culture* with clear understanding that it is the modern nomenclature of both the theory (*pariyatti*) and the practice *(patipatti)* of *samādhi.*

Samādhi is the second step of the Buddha's path of purification. A *dhammic* wayfarer, after rightly following the *sīla,* finds that his physical and vocal misdeeds are curtailed and minimized but they are not uprooted. It is due to the fact that the accelerating force, the mind still remains polluted and morally uncultured. The purity of physical and vocal deeds have just been brought under the mindful presence of abstinences. In the background of impurity of mind, there remains the possibility of its being polluted again. As such the purity of mind is essential.

How is it possible? It is possible through *samādhi*. 'See, O Monks, the root of the tree, the empty rooms, sit down and meditate, do not be repentant later on'. 'Sitting in the empty hall, meditating peacefully, there is the shower of divine happiness and also visualization of the nature of *Dhamma*'. 'Mind controlled thus, brings happiness—within and without'—are the emphatic expressions of the Buddha, which direct one to step forward to understand the mind, put a restraint over it and exert for *samādhi*. How? He first penetrates within and knows that—'Mind is the forerunner in all activities. All the physical, vocal and mental actions are chieftained by it. If one does something with a defiled mind, suffering follows him just like the wheels of a chariot to the feet of the horse. The activities, on the other hand, done with a mind trained and purified, bring happiness which follows him like a shadow.'[15] A man with a defiled mind is defiled and he, with purified mind, is pure. A spiritually trained mind is the source of happiness.[16] Therefore, making the mind free from defilements (*kileśa*), getting right understanding and tranquility followed by eternal bliss, there is the necessity of training of the mind and it is only possible through *samādhi*.

The term *samādhi* has three components, namely, *saṃ+ā+dhā*. The first two are the suffixes which respectively indicate the sense of 'properly and completely', and *dhā* stands for 'holding'. Thus holding properly and completely is the literal meaning of the term. Its technical meaning is the holding of moral consciousness together with its mental states properly and perfectly on a prescribed object. Therefore, *samādhi* is briefly described as one-pointedness of moral consciousness—'*Kusala-cittekaggatā Samādhi*'.[17]

It is evident from the text that mind is pure (luminous) by its nature and defiled with in-coming defiling elements.[18] With them there emerges a covering over it and it loses its own natural form. It becomes fickle, restless and unsteady.[19] It wanders here and there and creates attachment with various types of objects and indulges in sensual pleasure. More the amount of attachment, the greater is the degree of suffering.[20] Therefore, with an idea to remove the covering and bring it back to its natural form, one proceeds for the practice of meditation.

Here, one should first know the cause of the fickleness of mind. It is said that there are five hindrances which make the mind restless. They are called *nīvaraṇa.* They put obstacles and do not allow it to get concentrated on an object. They are the *kāmachanda, byāpāda, thina-middha, uddhacca-kukucca,* and *vicikicchā.*[21]

(i) *Kāma-chanda* is the name of the strong urge for sensual pleasure.
(ii) *Byāpāda* is ill will or antipathy. It is a kind of desire for doing harm to others. It appears while thinking about a man that he has done harm to him in the past, doing harm in the present and will do harm in the future or he has done harm to his near and dear ones in the past, doing harm in the present and will do harm in the future or he had helped his enemies in the past, helping them in the present and will help them in the future. Harbouring in this way the sense of antipathy, one thinks to do harm to others.
(iii) *Thina-middha* means sloth and torpor. Actually laziness connected with mental states is *thina* and the same connected with consciousness is *middha.*
(iv) *Uddhacca-kukucca* stands for worry and nervousness. In other words, it is the bewildering of mind and brooding over what is done and what is not done.
(v) *Vicikicchā* is the name of doubt. In ordinary sense, it is a state of mind full of perplexity. In technical sense, it is the doubt in the *Buddha, dhamma* and *saṅgha.*[22] As long as these hindrances are at work, it is very difficult to get concentration of mind.

The man, technically known as *yogāvacara,* makes efforts for suppression of these hindrances. It is possible with the arising of the *jhānangas,* the constituents or *jhāna*-factors.[23] They are five in number, namely, *vitakka, vicāra, pīti, sukha* and *ekaggatā.*[24]

(a) *Vitakka* means initial application of mind on the object. It is a kind of lifting of the consciousness and its concomitants and turning towards an object.[25]
(b) *Vicāra* is the sustaining of mind on the object. Therefore, it

is generally rendered as sustained application of mind.[26] The two *jhāna*-factors may be distinguished and better understood with the help of some similes.[27] Like alighting of a bee on a lotus is *vitakka* and *vicāra* is like humming around it. *Vitakka* is like the flapping of a bird before it flies and *vicāra* is like planning its movement. *Vitakka* is like the beating of a drum, and *vicāra* is like its reverberation.

(c) *Pīti* means a thrill of pleasant sensation. It is a type of joy or pleasurable interest. It is of five kinds,[28] namely, *khuddikāpīti, khanikāpīti, okantikā-pīti, ubbegāpīti* and *pharaṇāpīti. Kuddikāpīti* is the name of a thrill of pleasant sensation which makes the flesh click. *Khaṇikāpīti* is instantaneous joy which appears like the flash of lightning. *Okantipāpīti* is the flood of joy just like the breakers on the seashores. *Ubbegāpīti* is the name of transporting joy. It makes one able to float in the air. *Pharaṇāpīti* is the name of suffusing joy. It pervades just like the flood which overflows the small pond.

(d) *Sukha* is the name of happiness. It is a kind of pleasant feeling connected with the mind.[29] It is rather *somanassa* or the mental pleasant feeling. It may be understood that the *pīti* creates an interest in the object and *sukha* helps one in enjoying it. *Pīti* is the name of a joy which one gets in hope of realization of the object whereas *sukha* arises when the desert is realized.[30]

(e) *Ekaggatā* means one-pointedness. It makes the mind firmly fixed on the object. It, in other words, is the focusing of mind on the object.[31] It is like a steady lamp's flame in a windless place or like a firmly fixed pillar which never shakes by a strong wind. Thus each *jhāna*-factor has a definite function to do and with their effective role, the hindrances are suppressed.

The five hindrances are not the only impediments before concentration, there are others too. They are called *palibodha*.[32] They function as impediments in creating attachment with various objects as well as in developing sluggishness in the meditational efforts. They should be known and cut before proceeding for meditation. The text, in this context, enumerates ten major and five minor impediments. The major impediments are—the dwelling place (*āvāsa*), family (*kulaṃ*), gain (*lābho*) group of followers (*gaṇo*), construction work (*kammaṃ*), travel (*addhānaṃ*), relatives (*nāti*), affliction (*ābādho*), book (*gantho*) and supernatural power (*iddhi*). The minor impediments are the long hair on the head, body hair, nails, torn out robes, the bowl with a stain and unclean bed etc. One should severe these impediments by doing the needful in each case. The long hair on the head, body hair, nails etc. should be cut, the old robes be patched where necessary and dyed, the bowl having stain on it should be baked and the unclean bed etc. should be cleaned. In this way, being free from them, one should approach the *kalyāṇamitta* for having the suitable object for meditation, technically known as *kammaṭṭhāna*.

A *Kalyāṇamitta*[33] is a person who is wholly solicitous of welfare and helpful in spiritual progress. He is actually the most revered and dearly loved person. He is perfect in the theory and practice of meditation as well as in understanding the temperament of the persons concerned. In this way, according to the tradition, the Buddha is the best *kalyāṇamitta*. He should be approached for a suitable object for the pursuit of meditation, if he is alive. In his absence, his capable disciples, well-versed in theory and practice, should be approached. If such a person is not available in the place where one lives, he should go to the latter's place in a modest way, avoiding all sorts of discursive thoughts which may arise in the way either by themselves or in the company of the persons in his wayfaring. Reaching him, he should perform the normal duties and wait for a suitable moment for placing his request before him. He must not be in a hurry in expressing his desire but create favourable situation for his asking for a *kammaṭṭhāna*. The latter has a great responsibility in selecting the suitable *kammaṭṭhāna* for him. It should be fit for the temperament of the person concerned and helpful in his spiritual pursuit. Therefore, the study of the temperament is the first step in going for selecting of suitable *kammaṭṭhāna*. It is, however, determined by thorough examination of posture, action, food, marking the appearance and other mental and physical states occurring during the time of tests.[34]

For this purpose, the men are put into six divisions so far as their temperament is concerned. They are persons having a strong feeling of attachment (*rāgacarita*), of antipathy (*dosacarita*), having dullness and deception (*mohacarita*), having unwavering confidence (*saddhacarita*), possessing a rationalistic nature (*buddhicarita*), and having imaginative nature (*vitakkacarita*). It is a broad psychological analysis of the basic mental leanings which have been made to include all types of persons under these six heads.[35] The *kalyan-amitta,* in this background, ascertains the temperament of the person concerned and prescribes a *kammaṭṭhāna.*

The word *kammaṭṭhāna* is a technical term used for the object of meditation. It literally means the place of action. Here, action is restricted in the sense of *jhanic* actions. Therefore, the *kammaṭṭhāna* is the name of the place where *jhanic*-action is performed. He does not select anything as a *kammaṭṭhāna* but he selects one out of the forty *kammaṭṭhānas* already prescribed by the Buddha for the purpose. They are the ten circles (*kasiṇa),* ten stages of a dead body (*asubha*), ten objects of reflection (*anussati*), four illimitables (*appamaññā*), four formless objects (*āruppa*), one perception (*sanna*) and one analysis (*vavatthāna*).

A circle (*kasiṇa*) refers to a *kammaṭṭhāna* which is round in shape. It may be just like a ball. They are ten in number, namely: the *kasiṇas* made with clay, water, fire, air, of blue colour, of yellow colour and of red colour, of white colour, a hole and a light.[36] The ten *asubhas* refer to the ten stages of a dead body thrown under the sky in a cemetery or a place like that and receiving deformities due to natural and other forces. It denotes the loathsomeness of the forms of the dead body. They are ten in number: a bloated corpse, a discoloured corpse, a festering corpse, a disjoint corpse, a corpse eaten by vultures, jackals and other animals, a mangled corpse, a mutilated and mangled corpse, a corpse replete with blood, a worm infested corpse and a skeleton.[37]

The ten types of reflections are the reflections on the merits of the triple gems and other similar objects. They are the reflections on the *Buddha, dhamma, saṅgha,* morality, generosity, deities, peaceful calm, death, unclean things of our body and respiration.[38] The four illimitables are so named because the range of their practice is not limited. They can be extended over the infinite number of beings in all directions. They are friendliness, compassion, joy and equanimity.[39] The one perception (*saññā*) is the idea of the unpleasantness and loathsomeness about food.[40] The analysis (*vavatthāna*) is contemplating over and making analysis of the four basic material elements of which our body is composed.[41] The four formless objects (*āruppa*) are infinite space, infinite consciousness, nothingness and the state of the subtlest perceptions viz., neither perception nor non-perception.[42]

These are the forty types of *kammaṭṭhānas* prescribed by the Buddha for developing concentration of mind. The *kalyāṇamitta* selects any one of them, suitable to the temperament of the person concerned and advises him to proceed for meditation. It should also be known that the above forty types of *kammaṭṭhānas* are not suitable to all types of persons. They are given as stated above, according to their temperament.[43] It is based purely on a psychological analytic base. It is said in this context that the ten stages of a dead body and the unclean things in our body are the eleven objects which are suitable to a man having a strong feeling of attachment, technically known as *rāgacarita*. Any one of them is prescribed for such persons. They are to inculcate in him the sense of detachment marking the foulness of the body. Further, the four types of the illimitables and the four circles of blue, yellow, red and white colours are the objects suitable to the persons who have a strong feeling of antipathy known as *doṣacarita*. The reflection on breathing is suitable to such persons who are of a dull temperament (*mohacarita*). Again the reflection over the greatness of the *Buddha, dhamma, saṅgha*, merits of *sīla*, benevolence and the greatness of gods are the six reflections which are suitable to persons of believing temperament (*saddhācarita*). Reflections over death, the greatness of peaceful calm, perception and analysis are suitable to the persons of rationalistic nature (*buddhicarita*). There are ten more objects, namely: circles of earth, water, fire, air, gap, light and the four formless objects. They are suitable to persons of all temperaments. Therefore, the beginners start practising meditation on any one of such gross objects. However, there is one consideration in this process, that a gross object, bigger in size, is suitable to a person of dull temperament and object of a smaller size, is suitable to a man of imaginative or discoursive temperament.[44]

In this way, taking the object of meditation, one is advised to select a place for practice. First of all, he should see that he gets an opportunity to live in the same monastery with his teacher. Getting so he should start the practice of meditation under his guidance and do his duties towards him. If he does not get such an opportunity, he should select another monastery at a suitable distance. Living therein, when he finds some difficulties, he should approach his teacher in day time, generally after returning from the alms-round. He may even live with him for the night and return to his place the next day. However, his main concern is the development of concentration and for that a suitable place is the most essential factor. Therefore, he must avoid unfavourable places and select one which is congenial for the purpose.

According to the tradition, there are eighteen types of places which are regarded as unsuitable. They are—a large monastery, a monastery under construction, dilapidated monastery, a monastery situated on a highway, a monastery situated on a bank of a pond, a monastery which is surrounded by creepers or small tress having edible leaves, a monastery having flowers of beautiful colours, a monastery full of trees having delicious fruit, a famous monastery, a monastery in city, a monastery among timber, a monastery situated amidst arable fields, the monastery where there is the presence of incompatible persons, a monastery situated on the border of the countries, a monastery situated on the frontiers of a kingdom, a monastery where there are unsuitable objects and a monastery where there is the lack of *kalyāṇamitta.* These are the eighteen types of monasteries which are unfavourable for the development of concentration. One is advised to avoid such places and select one which is suitable for meditation.[45]

As the *yogāvacara* should be particular in avoiding a place which is not suitable, similarly, he should be alert in selecting a place which is suitable to bring harmony in proceeding for meditation. The suitable places for the purpose, according to the earlier texts, are the excluded dwelling, a forest, the foot of a tree, a mountain, an open field and a heap of straw. The *Viśuddhimagga* further makes a mention of the five qualities of a suitable place. It should be neither too far from the village nor too near it. It should be little frequented in the day and have no sound at night. There should not be disturbances with external elements like gladflies, wind, burning sun, and creeping creatures like serpents etc. It should be inhabited by learned monks, well-versed in theory and practice of the *dhamma.*[46] It appears from the description that the five qualities enumerated are in tune with the *middle path.* However, one should always be mindful of the core of the teachings of the Buddha that there should not be any attachment for the place. Therefore, the Buddha seems to be very much pleased with the forest life of monks as well as the dwelling at the foot of a tree. He has clearly stated that, 'These are the feet of trees, and these are empty places, meditate, be not slothful and remorseful later on.'[47]

After the selection of a suitable place for meditation, there should be the preparation of mind for the purpose. A congenial atmosphere should be prepared by developing the four-fold endeavour of not allowing the immoral states to arise which have not arisen, of the destruction of the immoral states which have already arisen, of allowing the arising of moral states which have not arisen and of helping the foster growth of the moral states which have come into existence. This prepares a congenial background in mind which should be followed with the practice of mindfulness.

The *yogāvacara*, after taking the *kammaṭṭhāna* suitable to his temperament either by himself or with the help of the teacher, should retire into solitude and make efforts for developing concentration. He should keep the *kammaṭṭhāna* before him at a reasonable distance, draw his mind from different directions and keep it at a distance, and fix it on the object. It is natural that a fickle mind does not remain on the object and keeps slipping away again and again. The *yogāvacara* must not be disturbed with it and be mindful and alert in arresting it and fixing it on the object.

After due practice, the five hindrances, technically called the *nīvaraṇas* are suppressed and become functionless. Following which there appear the constituents of *jhāna*, technically called *jhānagas*. Here it should be known that all the *jhāna*-factors do not suppress all hindrances. There is a process for this too. The one-pointedness (*ekaggatā*) suppresses sensual pleasure (*kāma-chanda*). The thrill of pleasant sensation (*pīti*) weakens ill-will (*byāpada*). The application of mind (*vitakka*) makes the sloth and torpor (*thina-middha*) without function. The composer (*sukha*) suppresses the distraction and worry (*uddhacca-kukucca*). Similarly, the sustained application of mind (*vicāra*) cuts the activities of doubt (*vicikicchā*). In this way the functions of the hindrances are suppressed and those of *jhāna*-factors start.

In this background, he makes efforts for the attainment of concentration. In the beginning, all the five constituents of *jhāna* are at work. The *vitakka* develops a leaning of mind towards the object. The *vicāra* holds it and keeps it sustained. *Pīti* generates a thrill of pleasant sensation within him and creates a joyful atmosphere for the attainment of the desert. The *sukha* brings composer both in mind and body. The *ekaggatā* functions in developing one-pointedness of mind on the object. In this way, with the help of the five *jhāna*-factors, the first stage of *rūpajhāna* is attained. It is technically called the *paṭhama-rūpajhāna* associated with the five *jhāna*-factors. It is the first achievement of the *yogāvacara* in his meditational endeavour. It generates confidence and the rays of hope in him for higher realization in his spiritual life.

In this context, the *yogāvacara* is advised not to be in a hurry in going for higher states. He should rather strengthen the first stage of *rūpajhāna* with five ways of mastering known as *āvajjanavasī, samāpajjanavasī, adhiṭṭhāna-vasī, uṭṭhana-vasī* and *paccavekkhana-vasi,*. *avajjana-vasī* is the mastery in adverting the mind. The *yogāvacara* adverts to the first stage of *rūpa-jhāna* wherever, whenever and as he wishes. *Samāpajjana-vasī* is the name of the mastery of entering into the *jhāna* quickly. He can enter within a span of time one takes to snap fingers or to wink. *Adhiṭṭhaña-vasī* is the mastery in remaining in the *jhāna* for the period he determines before entering in it. *Uṭṭhāna-vasī* is the name of mastery in emerging from the *jhāna*. He emerges from it exactly in the same moment as resolved by him. *Paccavekkhana-vasī* means the mastery in reviewing the *jhāna*. He reviews his previous *jhānic* proficiency and understands them as they have been mastered. Thus, the *yogāvacara* makes a survey of his *jhānic* achievement from the moment of starting to the moment of perfection and also from the moment of its perfection to the moment of its starting in ascending and descending order. In this way, he masters the first stage of *rūpajhāna* and makes it perfect.

After mastering the first stage of *rūpajhāna* in five ways and having the *jhanic* experience in him, he endeavours to attain a higher stage, technically known as the second stage of *rūpajhāna* (*dutiya-rūpajhāna*). In making such efforts, his mind is gradually trained. It is then not necessary for diverting towards the object. It is so trained that it naturally leans towards it. Therefore, in the second stage of *rūpajhāna,* the first *jhāna*-factor, *vitakka* becomes absent. There remain only four *jhāna* factors and with their association, the second stage of *rūpajhāna* is attained.[48] Here also, the *yogāvacara* does not hurriedly proceed for the attainment of higher stages but applies the same five ways of mastering. There comes a moment when he has a control on his mind and thereby gets concentration on the object.

Getting proficiency in obtaining the second stage of *rūpajhāna* the *yogāvacara* makes further efforts for the third stage. Here he finds that the mind is so trained that there is neither the need of applying it on the object nor that of sustaining on it. Therefore, at this stage the *vicāra* also becomes absent. There remain only three *jhāna* factors, namely, *pīti, sukha* and *ekaggatā.* Thus, he attains and dwells in the third stage of *rūpajhāna* associated with these three *jhāna*-factors.[49] Reaching this stage, the wandering tendency of mind is curtailed to a greater extent.

In going towards the attainment of the fourth stage of *rūpa-jhāna*, the function of *pīti* is also not essential. There is no need of generating joy in the hope of realization of the desired object, but it is by that time naturally realized. Thus *pīti* becomes absent in the fourth stage. There remain only two *jhāna*-factors, composer (*sukha*) and one-pointedness (*ekaggatā*). And with their association, the fourth stage or *rūpajhāna* is attained.[50]

With the attainment of the fourth stage of *rūapjhāna*, a sound background is prepared in mind for meditational achievement. Here, there is one point for consideration for the *yogāvacara*. With the presence of composer as *jhāna*-factor, both the mind and body are suffused with pleasant feeling. There is the possibility of developing a craving for this joyful and pleasant state. It is against the principle of meditation. Therefore, he becomes alert and replaces composer with another *jhāna*-factor, namely, indifference, (*upekkhā*). Thus, with the help of the two *jhāna*-factors, indifference and one-pointedness, he attains the fifth stage of *rūpajhāna*.[51] There is, then, the perfect concentration on the object but there is no affinity with it. There prevails indifference and provides the inner strength in getting concentration. Getting such proficiency in developing concentration is regarded as the highest achievement in the meditational pursuit. This is the landmark in the *jhānic* efforts of the *yogāvacara*. The mind becomes composed, clear, free from defilements, pliant and fit for higher spiritual activities.[52] There remains no disturbance at all and peace, tranquility, serenity and calm prevail. With such a mind, it is advised to enter into the stage of *vipassana*.

In this context, it should also be noted that all the five stages of *rūpajhāna* are attained on the same object. There is only the disappearance of the *jhāna*-factors in ascending order in accordance with the proficiency achieved in *jhānic* efforts. It should also be known here that the Suttantic tradition makes a mention of only four stages of *rūpajhāna*. It is said that all the five *jhāna*-factors remain present with the first stage of *rūpajhāna*. The first two, *vitakka* and *vicāra*, become absent in the second stage and there remain only three *jhāna*-factors. With them, the second stage of *rūpajhāna* is attained. In the third stage, *pīti* also becomes absent along with *vitakka* and *vicāra*. Only the two *jhāna*-factors, *sukha* and *ekaggatā* remain there. With their association, one attains the third stage of *rūpajhāna*. *Sukha* becomes absent in the fourth stage. It is replaced by indifference, and thus the fourth stage of *rūpajhāna* is attained with two *jhāna*-factors, indifference and one-pointedness. In this way the five stages of *rūpajhāna* as mentioned in the Adhidhammic tradition are reduced to four in the Suttantic one.[53]

After practising the different stages of *rūpajhāna*, the *yogāvacara* achieves proficiency in his mind in getting concentration on any object associated with form. No doubt, it is a marvelous achievement in his *jhānic* pursuit, yet, some more subtle stages are to be realized. Therefore, he makes efforts for developing concentration on the *arūpa*-object. Here, the word *arūpa* refers to an object which has neither colour nor form. And concentration developed on such an object is called *arūpa-jhāna*. It has four gradual stages of achievement.

There is a process of entering into *arūpajhāna* from the *rūpajhāna*. In the fifth stage of *rūpajhāna*, there was an object before the *yogāvacara* which he develops as to pervade all through. Wherever he sees, there is the pervading object. With the idea of going higher with his meditational power, he removes the object just like a curtain. As when a curtain is removed there is empty space, similarly, with the removal of all pervading objects associated with form, there appears infinite space before him. He takes it as an object and develops concentration on it. In due course of his practice, there comes a moment when his mind gets concentrated on such an object. This achievement is the first stage in the *arūpajhāna*, technically called *ākāsanañcāyatana*.[54]

After mastering the first stage, his mind becomes pliable for going higher. He mentally analyses the object before him and understands that it is his consciousness (*viññāṇa*) which embraces the infinite space. And therefore, it is real. Thinking so, he gives up the infinite space and takes infinite consciousness (*ananta-viññāṇa*) as an object for concentraton of his mind. He finds it more peaceful and calm than the previous one. He exerts and fixes his mind on it and develops concentration. After due practice and continuous efforts, he gets one-pointedness on it. This is the second achievement known as the *dutiya arūpajhāna* or *viññāṇancayatana*.[55]

The gradual proficiency in his *jhānic* pursuit encourages him to go higher. After making a thorough analysis of the nature of consciousness, he understands that it is void, empty and without reality; there is nothing in it. Thinking so, he gives up the infinite consciousness and takes up the nothingness of consciousness (*ākiñacañña*) as an object. It means that the infinite consciousness no longer remains as an object but is replaced by its nothingness. He starts thinking that there is nothing in it and continues so till his mind gets concentrated on the idea of nothingness. This is rather a replacement of his previous thought concerning the infinity of consciousness and arising of a new thought that there is nothing in it. He makes efforts for attaining single-mindedness and there comes a moment when he gets perfect concentration on it. It is the third achievement known as the third stage of *arūpajhāna* or *akiñcaññāyatana.*[56]

To master the third stage of *arūpajhāna*, the *yogāvacara* reflects on it again and again. He finds doing so dangerous, so far as perception is concerned, for neither perception-nor-non-perception appears to him peaceful and sublime. Thus, he takes it as an object and proceeds for developing concentration on it. After due practice and continuous endeavour, there develops one-pointedness and the complete absorption of mind on the object. This is the fourth and the last achievement in his *jhānic* pursuit, known as the fourth stage of *arūpajhāna* or *nevasaññānasaññāyatana.*[57]

In this context, it should be remembered that with all the four stages of *arūpajhāna*, there constantly remain two *jhāna* factors; indifference (*upekkhā*) and single-mindedness (*ekaggatā*). The object in each stage is different. Because of the association of these two *jhāna*-factors in all the four stages, they are regarded as similar to that of the fifth stage of *rūpajhāna.* There, in the *sāmaññaphalasutta,* there is the mention of the four stages of *rūpajhāna* as the pre-requisite, of entering into *vipassanā.* The *poṭṭhapādasutta,* however, presents the descriptions of *rūpa-jhāna* and *arūpa-jhāna* in ascending order. Similar descriptions are available in the *abhidhammika* texts too. Therefore, it appears that both the traditions were prevalent side by side in the early days.

The practice of *samādhi* has a definite aim and that is the preparation of mind for realization of right understanding (*paññā*). As the practice of the *sīla* is for *samādhi,* similarly, the practice of *samādhi* is for realization of *paññā* which culminates in realization of *nibbāna.* Besides, there are some mundane achievements too and one of them is the attainment of intuitional knowledge (*abhiññā*). It is achieved because of the subtle mind. The fifth stage of *rūpajhāna* is regarded as the pre-requisite for the practice of *abhiññā*. It is of five types; namely, psychic power (*iddhividha*), divine ear (*dibbasota*), divine eye (*dibbacakkhu*), penetration into the mind of others (*paracittavi jānana*) and the knowledge of past existence (*pubbenivāsa-nusatiñāṇa*). With psychic power, one becomes capable of performing various types of wonderous activities, such as, being one he becomes many, and being many becomes one; he becomes visible and invisible at his will; he passes through the walls and mountains etc., dives in and emerges from the earth as in the water; walks on water as on earth and so on.[58] Divine ear is the attainment of a kind of proficiency through which he hears the sound of far and near, both worldly and divine.[59] Divine eye refers to a kind of proficiency of having a vision without speciotemporal barrier. He can see the things of far and near as he wishes. He also sees the beings coming into existence and passing away into different planes of existence according to their moral and immoral activities.[60] By penetrating into the mind, he understands the thought of others. The state of mind affected with delusion, exalted or unexalted, are clearly known by him.[61] Having the power of knowledge of past existence, he knows with minute details the planes and the states of existence, where he was born on the basis of his moral or immoral activities. He remembers his numerous births, even up to the many cycles of evolution and dissolution of the universe.[62] In this way, one gets five types of super-knowledge after the attainment of the *abhiññā*. However, it has been clearly stated by the Buddha that it is a mundane achievement and, therefore, it should be understood as an impediment for spiritual progress. Therefore, it is advisable for the *yogāvacara* not to pay heed to such achievements. Understanding them as impediments, he should proceed further for realization of *paññā* (right understanding) for going further for the attainment of *nibbāna*, the state of eternal bliss.

SOCIAL CULTURE (*BRAHMA-VIHĀRA*)

Appearance of the Buddha is for the happiness of all. He has before him an universal problem, a definite goal and a path existing between the two. The problem is the suffering of mankind, the goal is attainment of a state of eternal bliss and the path is a psycho-ethical process of gradual purification. Throughout his active life for forty-five years, he is seen as a wayfarer making righteous wandering (*cārikā*) through the villages, towns and cities of the country and preaching the *dhamma* for the well-being of all. During the course of his such wandering and in the background of ripe experience, he introduced an ideal, known as *brahma-vihāra*; a sublime way of living. It manifests itself in two ways as a psycho-ethical thought and a noble attitude of *social behaviour.* As a thought, it is the law of gradual harmonization and generation of ecstatic joy; and as a practice, it is the application of four virtues. The two function together as the two wheels of a chariot and consummate in springing up of a universal social order, non-violent in character and saturated with peace and tranquility, within and without. This, we name as the dawn of social culture.

The term *brahma-vihāra* has two component parts, namely, *brahma* and *vihāra. Brahma* means superior, noble, excellent, sublime etc. *Vihāra* literally means living, dwelling, going on with four-fold modes of functioning as standing, sitting, lying down and moving. Traditionally, it refers to a state of living with ecstatic joy. In its technical sense, it expresses the fact of a state of living with complete awareness towards the body, feeling, consciousness and the nature of *dhamma.* In the present context, it exhibits the sense of a way of living with the four noble virtues. Thus the two terms *brahma* and *vihāra* are indicative of a sublime way of living with the four noble virtues. They are friendliness (*mettā*), compassion (*karuṇā*), joy (*muditā*) and equanimity (*upekkhā*). These four states are inculcated, nourished and developed in a balanced way so as to pervade and embrace all the beings, just like the soothing touch of the pleasant wind. It is done through a practice known as *brahma-vihāra-bhāvanā.*

The practice has a pre-requisite to be performed. It is the preparation of mind. As for a proper sowing of a seed, the preparation of the ground is a necessary condition, so also for the proper plantation of these virtues, cultivation of mind is essential as the first condition. It is done by developing a number of qualities. It is said that 'he should be straight-forward, mild, humble, satisfied, man of right speech, and restrained sense. He should have limited number of activities, attitude of leading life nicely with limited facilities, and even in unfavourable situations. He should restrain his physical, vocal and mental activities and not develop extra attachment towards the family and their belongings. Weeding out in this way the basic impediments, he should make the mind pliable and receptive to practice the four-fold *brahma-vihāra.*

How it should be done? It should be understood that the four sublime virtues, friendliness, compassion, joy and equanimity, are the naturally gifted virtues with each person. They are available as moral psychic factors together with a number of other moral and immoral ones. They remain either dormant or active due to the forces of immoral or moral resultants or bewildered due to the functioning of variegated mental forces. In this situation, they should be identified, made object of consciousness and gradually developed. But how?

(i) *Friendliness* (*mettā*): It is the name of the moral volition of well-being of all (*hitesitā parahita-kāmatā*).[63] It is the boundless extension of friendly consciousness from self (*sva*) to all (*sabba*). All the beings become its object. There is none who remains untouched with its soothing wave. The practice proceeds as—'whatever beings there are, either moving or remaining in one place, either long or great, middle-sized or short, small or large; either already born, or seeking birth; either living in lower planes of existence or in those of the higher ones or existing in the middle of a vacuum; may all be happy, may all be free from enmity, devoid of ill will, and away from all kinds of disturbances. Let their wayfaring be smooth and full of happiness.' 'As a mother protects her only son even at the cost of her life, so also let every one cultivate a boundless friendly consciousness towards all being.' With such infinite friendly consciousness, one should dwell making all the directions filled, saturated and touched within and without.[64] In the situation, there is the radiation of the waves of friendliness from one individual to other and they embrace all the beings without any discrimination. The feeling of ill-will towards all beings is minimized and finally uprooted—*Mettaṃ hi bhāvanaṃ bhāvayato yo byāpado, so pahīyissati.*[65] All the beings of different temperament become friendly and there remains no enemy in any of the directions. As such there is no chance for the functioning of the feeling of ill-will, violence at all:

Mettāya mitte majjhatte, verika vā yathākkamaṃ, Karonto sīmasambhedaṃ, attani va samaṃ phare.
Bhūmi-desa-disā sattā, bhedabhinnesu odhiso,
Yathāsambhavamappeti, Sabbasattesavā- nodhiso.[66]

There is a similar wave of friendliness with friends, with those of indifferent ones and also with them who are enemies. The boundary of a particular place, country, or direction is broken and removed. Everyone is within the soothing touch of friendliness. The term *byāpadavā* or one who possesses ill-will, antipathy and hatred disappears.[67]

(ii) *Compassion* (*karuṇā*): It is the name of a moral volition for eradication of suffering of others. It is not a simple verbal expression towards beings in suffering but a positive attitude to be one with the suffering of others and to make right efforts for its gradual minimization—(*para-dukkhe sati hadaya-kampanaṃ; kiṇāi vā para-dukkhaṃ, hiṃsati, vināseti ti attho*). Here the beings in suffering of all planes of existence are its objects (*dukkhī janesu karuṇā*). The beings of the past and those of the future do not come in its purview. It embraces the beings of the present state of existence; maybe the friends, enemies and those who are indifferent. There is no barrier of the place and the status of beings.

The practice of compassion proceeds in the same way as that of friendliness. Whatever beings in suffering there are; big or small, long or short, moving or remaining in one place, staying far or near, seen or unseen, maybe free from suffering; maybe free from all kinds of ailments, fear, disturbance, misfortunes etc. Let there be a happy and fearless wayfaring in their life. Practising in this way, one develops the range of compassion to pervade all the directions and make them saturated with its soothing wavelets. The radiation of compassion-wavelets proceeds from one individual to the other and consummates in positive efforts for the eradication of suffering. The annoyance and hatred towards such beings is reduced and in due course uprooted—*Karuṇam bhāvanaṃ bhāvayato, yā vihesā sā pahīyissati.*

The *nāma-rūpa-pariccheda* further proceeds with description of the *karuṇā-bhāvanā* as:—Why the beings should tremble with fear? Why the disturbing forces are creating an unpleasant situation with beings? Why beings are seen in a state of helplessness? Why they are driven forcefully to misfortune? Why they are surrounded with fear just like a bird thrown in the fearful circle of wind? Let their suffering of variegated, nature be eradicated, agonies be destroyed, sinful activities be minimized, fear be reduced, pollutions and impediments be done away. Let there be the dawn of rays of hope of getting freedom from all kinds of unpleasantness etc. Compassion with such consciousness helps one to penetrate into the suffering of others and exerts for its eradication. It is said:

Iccevaṃ anukampanto, sabba-satte ti sabbathā,
sabba-dukkha-samugghātaṃ, patthento-karuṇāyati.[68]

(iii) *Joy* (*muditā*): It is the name of a volition, moral in nature, of experiencing unalloyed joy on the prosperity of others (*sukhitesu muditā*). It is seen that the people finding one in a state of establishment with happiness start developing jealousy towards him. This destroys the individual and social harmony. Here, there is the replacement of 'jealousy' by unmixed pleasure to see the prosperous situation and happy state of existence of all beings. As a mother whose child is healthy, educated, well-placed and prosperous feels unalloyed joy, similarly, there should be the development of a state of joyfulness towards others. One develops the practice, goes on nourishing this sublime virtue and makes all the directions saturated with it. By doing so, the feeling of aversion is reduced:- *Muditaṃ bhāvanaṃ bhāvayato yā arati sā pahīyissati.*

The practice of joy is further elaborated as:—'It is nice, it is pleasant that the beings in human world as well as in divine worlds are rejoicing. How joyful it is that they have achieved the state of accomplishment of their purposes and cherished desires. The beings with their mirthful and soothing appearance, fulfilled wishes, surrounded with boundless thrill of pleasant sensations and bliss may live long and have more and more rejoicement'.

Bhayamaggamatikkantā, Dukkha-saṅkhāra-nissaṭā,
khemaggamanuppattā, phītasampatti-phullitā.
Samagga-sahitā cesā, patisanthāra-pesalā,
sampattiṃ, abhivādenti, kalyāṇa-guṇa-bhūsitā.
Iti sammā piyāyanto, sukhādhigama-sampadaṃ,
sattānaṃ abhirocento, muditāya samaṃ pharaṃ.[69]

(iv) *Equanimity* (*upekkhā*): The term *upekkhā* is used here in a technical sense. It does not convey the sense as it is understood in generic and ordinary parlance. It rather expresses the sense of detachment, unaffectedness, untrembleness, indifference etc. It is a moral volitional effort for maintaining equanimity in all situations. A man, in the process of his life, may have occasions of gain or loss, fame or defame, criticism or praise, pleasure or pain etc. These are the natural phenomena of life (*loka-dhamma*). Their coming into being is an unavoidable process. Realizing it as such, one should not be affected with them and develop the attitude of a mountain as it is marked in respect to forceful wind from any direction.[70] He should develop the practice-oriented behaviour like earth, water, fire and air.[71] When the situation is like this, why one should create a disturbed state of mind? Rather, giving up the intense feeling of liking one and disliking the other with a balanced and detached mind, one would proceed for the well-being of all. When this virtue is developed in this way, the functional aspects of the desire to develop extra coveteousness (*visama-lobha*) and the strong sense of hatred (*visama-dosa*) are gradually reduced. In short, the destructiveness is minimized and gradually eradicated—*Upekkhaṃ bhāvanaṃ bhāvayato, yo paṭigho so pahīyissati.*[72]

The other meaning of *upekkhā* is the developing indifference towards the folly of others and exerting for its removal. One may have association with such persons in day-to-day life who behave unpleasantly due to their ignorance. One should not be affected with their wrongful behaviour and make right efforts for gradual removal of their ignorance. The text suggests that:

Iti sankhāyapekkhanto, hita-kāmo pi pāṇino,
Apakkhapātupekkhāya, samaṃ pharati yoniso.[73]

The third meaning of *upekkhā* is the *samatā*, a balanced state of mind towards all types of men, friends, enemies, indifferent ones etc. It destroys the attitude of discrimination and develops the state of *samadarśana.* The text exhibits it as:

Attani mitte majjhatte, verike ti catusvapi,
Karonto sīmasambhedaṃ, sabbattha sama-mānasaṃ.

The practice of the four virtues goes simultaneously, though in different moments of consciousness. They should become a part of our being and there should not be such moments when these virtues are not harboured in mind and manifested through three doors of action, namely physical door, vocal and mental door. Awareness at these doors should be a constant fact.[74]

The four sublime virtues have their individual as well as collective impact. Individually, friendliness destroys *byāpāda* (ill-will), compassion eradicates *vihesā* (hatred, annoyance), joy reduces *arati* (aversion) and equanimity minimizes *paṭigha* (the functional attitude of harming etc.).[75] The four, in their collective effort, weaken, reduce and destroy the forces disturbing social harmony. With minimization of such forces, there is gradual emergence of the state of harmony like—*hiri* (feeling shame at the moment of doing something immoral), *otappa* (honour for the society), *alobha* (sacrifice), *pattidāna* (sharing of spiritual gains), *diṭṭhi-ujukaraṇa* (giving up the wrong notions), *ujukatā* (straight-forwardness) etc. In the background of their balanced functioning, there is the possibility of emergence of a social order, non-violent in nature and saturated with peace and tranquility.[76]

NOTES AND REFERENCES

1. *K.N.* 1, 32.
2. *A.S.* 27.
3. *M.V.* 13.
4. *K.N.* 1, 189, 255
5. *M.V.* 3.
6. *D.N.* 2, 45–51; *M.V.* 3; *K.N.* 1, 63.
7. *D.S.* 3–146; A. 3–21; *A. San.* 1–39.
8. *A. Saṅ.* 69–75, 114–155.
9. *Tato parañca paṭisandhādayo rathācakkamiva yathākkamaṃ eva parivattantā pavattanti.*
   Patisandhibhavaṅgavīthiyo, Cuti ceha tathābhavantare,
   Punasandhibhavangamiccayaṃ, parivattati cittasantati.
10. *Tattha tayo addhā, dvādasangāni, Visatākārā, tisandhi, catusaṇkhepā, tīṇi vaṭṭāni, dve mūlāni ca Veditabbāni.*
11. *Atite hetavo pañca, idāni phalapañcakaṃ,*
    Idāni hetavo pañca, āyatiṃ phalapañcakaṃ. (*A. San.* 214–215)
12. *S.N.* 2, 153
13. *M.N.* 2, 210–11.
14. *Sīle patiṭṭhāya naro sapañño, cittaṃ paññaṃ ca bhāvayaṃ,*
    Ātāpī nipako bhikkhu, so imaṃ vijaṭaye jaṭaṃ ti, (*S.N.* 1, 14, 165)
15. *K.N.* 1, 17.
16. *Dantaṃ cittaṃ sukhāvahaṃ* (*K.N.* 1, 20.).
    Dantaṃ guttaṃ rakkhitaṃ saṃvuttaṃ mahato atthāya bhavissati (*A.N.* 1.10).
17. *V.M.* 57.
18. *A.N.* 1.10.
19. *K.N.* 1. 20.
20. *Yesaṃ sataṃ piyāni, sataṃ dukkhāni, . . . yesaṃ ekaṃ piyaṃ ekaṃ dukkhaṃ* (*K.N.* 1, 175).
21. *D.S.* 258–60.
22. *D.S.* 258–59.
23. . . . *Yathā īṇaṃ, yathā rogaṃ, yathā bandhanāgāraṃ, yathā dāsabyaṃ, yathā kantārāddhānamaggaṃ; evaṃ ime pañca nīvaraṇe appahīne attani samanupassati, yathā āṇanyaṃ yathā-ārogyaṃ, yathā bandhanāmokkhaṃ, yathā khemantabhūmi, evameva, ime pañca nivaraṇe pahīne attani samanupassati* (*D.N.* 1.50–51).
24. *D.S.* 47–51.
25. *Appanālakhaṇo vitakko* (*M.P.* 65); *ārammaṇe cittassa abhiniropanalakkhāṇo* (*A.S.* 94).

26. *Anujjanalakkhaṇo vicāro*—*M.P.* 64; *arammaṇānumajjanlakkano* (*A.S.* 95).
27. *M.P.* 65; *A.S.* 44–95.
28. *A.S.* 95.
29. *Somanassa-vedanāya etaṃ nāma* (*A.S.* 96).
30. *Kantārakhinnassa vanantodakadassnasavanesu viya pīti, vanacchyappaveasudakaparibhogamiva sukhaṃ.* (*A.S.* 66)
31. *Pāmokkhalakkhaṇo ca samādhi* (*A.S.* 97).
32. *V.M.* 61.
33. *Piyo garu bhāvanīyo, vattā ca vacanakkhamo,*
Gambhiraṃ ca kathākattā no caṭṭhane niyojaye (*V.M.* 66).
34. *Iriyāpathato kicca-bhojanā-dissanādito.*
Dhammappavattito ceva, cariyāyo vibhavaye ti (*V.M.* 71).
35. *V.M.* 69.
36. *V.M.* 74.
37. *V.M.* 75.
38. *V.M.* 75.
39. *Mettā karuṇā muditā upekkhāti ime cattāro Brahmavihārā* (*V.M.* 75).
40. *Āhāre paṭikulasaññā ekā sañña* (*V.M.* 75).
41. *Catudhātu-vavaṭṭhānaṃ ekaṃ vavatthānaṃ* (*V.M.* 75).
42. *V.M.* 75.
43. *Sabbaṃ cetaṃ ujuvipaccanīkavasena ca atisappayavasena ca vuttaṃ* (*V.M.* 77).
44. *V.M.* 77.
45. *Mahāvāsaṃ Navāvasāṃ, jarāvasaṃ ca panthanī.*
Sondiṃ paṇṇañca pupphaṃ ca, phalaṃpatthitamevaca,
Nagaraṃ dāruṅā, khettaṃ, visabhagena pattanaṃ,
Paccantasīmasappayaṃ, yattha mitto na labbhati (*V.M.* 77).
46. *V.M.* 82.
47. *Etāni, Cunda, rukkhamūlāni, etani suññagārani, jhāyatha, Cunda, mā Pamadattha, mā pacchāvipaṭisārino ahuvattha* (*M.N.* 1.61).
48. *D.S.* 48–49.
49. *D.S.* 48–49.
50. *D.S.* 49.
51. *D.S.* 50.
52. *So evaṃ samāhite citte parisuddhe pariyodāte anaṅgaṇe vigatupakkilese mudubhūte kammanīye thite ānejappatte ñāṇdassanāya cittṃ, abhinīharati abhininnameti* (*D.N.* 1.67).
53. *D.N.* 1.65–67.
54. *D.S.* 73; 1. 153; *V.M.* 226.
55. *D.S.* 73; *D. N.* 1. 153; *V.M.* 227.
56. *D.S.* 73; *D. N.* 1. 154; *V.M.* 228.
57. *D.S.* 73; *D. N.* 1. 154; *V.M.* 238.
58. *D.N.* 1. 68.
59. *D.N.* 1. 69.
60. *D.N.* 1. 72.
61. *D.N.* 1. 70.
62. *D.N.* 1. 71.
63. *Yā sattesu mettā*—*mettacetouimutti.* (*V.* 337).
Tāva mejjatiti mettā, sinihayatīti attho. (*V.M.* 216).

Ye keci pāṇabhūtatthi, Tasā vā thāvarā vā anavasesā,
Dighā vā ye mahantā vā, majjhimā rassakā aṇukathūlā.
Diṭṭhā vā ye ca adiṭṭhā, ye ca dūre vasanti avidūre.
Bhūta va sambhavesī vā, sabbe sattā bhavantu sukhitattā. (*K.N.* 1. 280–81).
Sabbe sattā, sabbe pāṇā, sabbe bhūtā, sabbe puggalā, sabbe attabhāva-pariyāpannā, averā, abyānajjha, anighā, sukhena attānaṃ pariharantu. (*P.M.* 2. 13).

64. *Mettāsaha gatena cetasā ekaṃ disaṃ pharitvā viharati, taṭthā, dutiyaṃ, tathā tatiyaṃ tatha catutthaṃ, iti uddhaṃ adho tiriyaṃ sabbadhi sabbattatāya sabbavantaṃ lokaṃ mettāsahagatena cetasā vipulena mahaggatena appamāṇena averena abyapajjena pharitvā viharati* (*V.* 326).
65. *M.N.* 2. 104.
66. *N.R.P.* 138–39.
67. *Yena rāgena, yena dosena, yena mohena, byāpadavā assa, so rago doso moho pahiṇo, ucchinnamūlo, anabhāvaṃkato, āyatiṃ anuppādadhammo.* (*M.N.* 2, 40–41).
68. *N.R.P.* 140.
69. *N.R.P.* 142.
70. *Selo yathā ekaghano, vātena na samīrati,*
    Evaṃ nindā–pasansāsu, na samijjanti panḍitā (*K.N.* 1. 25)
71. *M.N.* 2, 101–4.
72. *M.N.* 2, 41.
73. *N.R.P.*, 143.
74. *Titthaṃ caraṃ nisinnaṃ vā,*
    Sayāno vā yāvatassa vigatamiddho.
    Etaṃ satiṃ adhiṭṭheyya,
    Brahmametaṃ vihāraṃidhamāhu. (*K.N.* 1. 291)
75. 'Mātā vạ̄ dahare putte, gilāne yobbanaṭṭhite,
    Sakiccapasute ceva, catudhā sampavattati'. (*N.R.P.* 144)
76. *Iccetā pana bhāvento, pasannamukhamānaso,*
    Sukham supati sutto pi, pāpaṃ kiñcina passati. (*N.R.P.* 143)

4

Causality, Cardinality and Conditioned Reality

RAJA RAMANNA

INTRODUCTION

Early Buddhist philosophy has much in common with scientific philosophy, a fact referred to by Bertrand Russell and many other scholars of philosophy. A more detailed work on the logic of the Buddhists is by Stcherbatsky.[1] It is divided into two volumes entitled *Buddhist Logic.* The first volume is devoted to the commentary on Buddhist logic and the other gives the original works translated from the Sanskrit dating up to the sixth century AD.

From these works, one gets an idea of the standpoint of early Buddhism and the meaning of the words 'conditioned reality', 'nothingness' (*śūnyatā*), the creative void out of which everything comes into existence, and *kṣaṇa* (instant) and all these have a relevance to modern physics though it is not very well known in western countries.

Early Buddhism does not depend on a God or the existence of a soul. The whole universe depends only on the laws of causality, be it in the material world or the moral sphere. We now know that the former is controlled by the laws of physics and according to early Buddhism, the latter is controlled by a well-regulated life, also determined by causal laws and defined by the Buddha himself in what is known as the 'eight-fold path'. Since no God is postulated, something else is required to take its place. Thus causality and causal relations become matters of prime importance.

It is the purpose of this essay not only to show the relevance of these older works, but also to demonstrate how they can unify much of the foundations of physics and even give quantitative results which are in full agreement with quantum mechanics as we know it. In this way, Buddhist logic may throw some light on the problems confronting the foundations of quantum mechanics.

By 'conditioned reality', we mean that all our thoughts, actions and observations (TAO for short), depend on something or everything else and there is nothing which has an independent existence. It is, however, possible that certain events take place due to the operation of certain causes whose relation to other causes may not matter, but in general, all recognizable TAOs are conditioned by a very large number, if not an infinite number of other factors. Later, we make use of these concepts to derive values of physical quantities.

The concept of 'nothingness' is profound and is due to the logician of the second century AD, Nāgārjuna. Many books have been written about him and it is remarkable how close his writings come to recent publications in physics, especially the book entitled '*Something Called Nothing'—Physical Vacuum, What is it?*[2] This book points out that the vacuum state is the fundamental one for the beginning of all physical activities by the formation of virtual states. Nāgārjuna, from a purely logical exposition points out that this can be the only possible picture of creative and physical processes. We make no further reference to the theory of nothingness as it is required only marginally in these considerations. Besides, sufficient literature already exists on the works of Nāgārjuna.[3]

The theory of '*kṣaṇa*' is a statement of the concept of 'instant' over whose average values, causes and effects can be quantified. Since this is a commonly accepted notion of time averages, it is not proposed to discuss it in detail but their full implications are given in Stcherbatsky's work already referred to.

CONDITIONED REALITY

Let $A_1, A_2 \ldots\ldots A_n \ldots\ldots$, be the various TAOs and $a_{11}, a_{12}, a_{13} \ldots\ldots$ etc. be the various conditions which generate the TAO, e.g., A_1 takes place when conditions $a_{11}, a_{12}, a_{13} \ldots\ldots a_{1n}$ exist. We write all possibilities in matrix form as follows:

Thoughts, Actions and Observations (TAO)	*Sequence of Conditions*					
A_1	a_{11}	a_{12}	a_{13}	–	a_{1n}	–
A_2	a_{21}	a_{22}	a_{23}	–	a_{2n}	–

Thoughts, Actions and Observations (TAO)	*Sequence of Conditions*						
–	–	–	–	–	–	–	.... (1)
A_n	a_{n1}	a_{n2}	a_{n3}	–	a_{nn}	–	etc.

The values of the a's can be 1 or 0 depending on whether the condition is relevant to that particular TAO.

In order to convert the above matrix to represent actual physical quantities and be able to interpret them as physical laws, we invoke the Cantor diagonal construction which Cantor used in showing the difference between the various types of infinities, particularly between countable and non-countable infinity. The theory in itself is a mathematical differentiation between continuous and discrete quantities. It can also be made the starting point for the foundations of quantum mechanics since it deals with physical quantities, which under certain conditions are discrete and in others continuous.

It will be recalled that Cantor proved that if we measure all the points on a continuous line, there are not enough integers to count them all. The method can further be used to prove the celebrated Godel Theorem on Incompleteness.

The Cantor diagonal method consists of writing all the points on a line lying, say between 0 and 1 (or in any continuous interval) in decimal notation. Let $S_0\ S_1 \ldots S_n \ldots$ be points on a straight line. We can presume that we can continuously count all the points by taking the decimals to an infinite number.

$$S_0 = 0.X_{00}\, X_{01}\, X_{02}\, X_{03} \ldots\ldots\ldots X_{0n} \ldots\ldots\ldots$$

$$S_1 = 0.X_{10}\, X_{11}\, X_{12}\, X_{13} \ldots\ldots\ldots X_{1n} \ldots\ldots\ldots$$

$$S_2 = 0.X_{20}\, X_{21}\, X_{22}\, X_{23} \ldots\ldots\ldots X_{2n} \ldots\ldots\ldots$$

....

....

$$S_n = 0.X_{n0}\, X_{n1}\, X_{n2}\, X_{n3} \ldots\ldots\ X_{nn} \ldots\ldots\ldots$$

....

....

It will, however, be noticed that a number, say S, will not be found in the enumeration if S is created such that

$$S \neq 0.X_{00} X_{11} X_{22} X_{33} \ldots\ldots\ldots X_{nn} \ldots\ldots\ldots$$

This is because the particular diagonal element will always be different by definition. This demonstrates that if one tries to enumerate all the points continuously, there are an infinite number of missing entries showing that a countable ∞ is different from a non-countable ∞.

This method can be used to determine the missing TAO from matrix (1) for each diagonal. There will be in principle n! missing sequences. If for some reason, the events are all ordered, there will be only one such sequence.

After having shown the existence of two kinds of infinities, Cantor went on to show that an infinite number of infinities can be formed by what is known as the Cantor Continuum. The method consists of showing that from a set of positive integers, it is possible to construct another set of integers with a different cardinal number.[4] If a set A consists of three integers {1, 2, 3}, a set B can be constructed—{1, 2, 3,}, {1, 2,}, {1, 3,}, {2, 3,}, {1}, {2}, {3}, and 0 i.e., with eight different elements. As it is shown later, this continuum property can be used to get the levels of atoms if a proper correspondence is made. Cantor has in general shown that a set with n elements can generate another set with 2^n elements of a different cardinal number.

Further, if we interchange the rows, there will be a different ordering of the conditional sequences and for each of these sets of sequences there will be a different sequence of the non-diagonal elements, not found among the rows.

From these very general considerations, we proceed to consider the special case where the matrix elements are physical entities. In such a system, we can replace TAO by the word 'events'.

We consider the following three cases where:

1. the number of conditions and the events are finite and for every event there is the same number of conditions i.e., we consider only square matrices;
2. the ordering of the sequences could change depending on the nature of reality. This could come about as a result of space-time. It may also happen that the number of sequence conditions and the number of events though finite, may not necessarily be equal. This could happen if the number of

events generated by a sequence of conditions is more than one, or a number of sequences generate the same event; and
3. the number of events and associated conditions are both noncountably infinite (continuous). This could happen if the values of the a's are not only restricted to 1 and 0, but could have values continuously between 0 and 1.

As an example of how matrix (1) can be interpreted, we consider the case where there exists a sequence consisting of only 1's. If the various other sequences are also arranged in such a manner that all the diagonal elements are 1's, the missing sequence will be only 0's. This means that there is no event when there are no conditions. Similarly, if the missing sequence is all 1's, it means that there is no event which requires all the conditions to exist. Such cases do not present themselves in actual situations.

NEWTONIAN PHYSICS

Newtonian physics depends on equations of motion and initial boundary conditions, from which all information about a system can be obtained. We can therefore assume that in a classical system, there is a point to point correspondence between a finite number of causes and events.

Further, in Newtonian physics there is an absolute co-ordinate system to which all things can be referred to and velocities of infinite magnitude are permitted. Causality means that an event cannot take place before the cause. The event, however, can be observed at different points separated from each other at great distances, instantaneously, e.g., Newtonian gravitation.

In Newtonian physics, time is an irreversible parameter absolutely separated from space. If events follow a certain time sequence, then the various entries of sequences in the matrix will follow a certain order, as a result of which only one sequence will be missing due to the diagonal effect. One could, in principle, attribute it to time irreversibility.

In physical problems where time dependence is involved, the ordering of the sequence of matrix elements is as important as the ordering of the sequences that define causality. Since causality implies that under no circumstances the event should precede the cause, it reduces the number of possibilities of the various diagonal sequences to one.

RELATIVISTIC PHYSICS

In classical physics, space and time are separate entities, but the basis of the Buddhist approach is to recognize the dependence of one on the other. If, therefore, space-time is taken as an integrated four-dimensional entity, it will be seen that Case 2 will seem closer to the truth.

Case 2 is essentially a special case of Case 1 except that in Case 2, there is no absolute reference system of co-ordinates and physical laws are invariant in space-time. The very assumption of space-time implies the existence of a universal finite limiting velocity which in the Theory of Relativity is that of light.

In such systems, there are many events which satisfy causality but do not necessarily have a time sequence. Besides, there could be many events arising from only one sequence of conditions or vice-versa there may be many sequences which lead to the same event. This is in agreement with the Theory of Relativity where, though causality is not disturbed, events which are neither the cause nor the result of one another, have no time-order and a reversal of time-order is also possible.[5] This is possible if the events are in different light cones.

In our matrix terminology, it means that because of space-time, the sequence order can be changed and the same set of conditions can produce different events.

QUANTUM PHYSICS

In quantum mechanics, we have a very different kind of theory. Events are described by astract wave functions whose interpretation depends on probability considerations.

The Uncertainty Principle further adds to the complexity of defining the conditions for an event. Even this is not established until a measurement is made and digested by the observer with a consciousness. Quantum mechanics predicts the existence of not only observable states which can be measured, but predicts the existence of virtual states in vacuum i.e., in nothingness.

In this present matrix formulation, because of the existence of quantized parameters, wave particle duality and of virtual states, the matrix elements could have the following possibilities:

(a) The matrix elements could have values continuously between 0 and 1. This could come about due to averaging effect over time or as a result of the influence of other parameters;

(b) The Cantor diagonal construction can also be applied to the other diagonal perpendicular to it and the same considerations can refer to rows. Here each row refers to a specific condition which requires to be satisfied for a certain set of events.

(c) In general, the differential equation provides causal relations in classical and quantum mechanics. In quantum mechanics, the solution of the Schrödinger equation depends on the type of boundary conditions one imposes on it. Some quantities get quantized while others remain in a continuum. For example, for a particle in a box, energy is quantized while position remains in a continuum. Thus their cardinality is different. We have from Cantor's Theory of the Continuum that n entries from a lower cardinality will have for the next higher cardinality 2^n entries.

Possibility (a) which suggests that matrix element values can be between 0 and 1 implies that the matrix elements are changing in time in a random manner (*kṣaṇa* theory). We will not specify how this happens but note that these values come about as some time average. The very fact that the values of the matrix elements are continuous implies that it is a non-countable set. It also implies that there are an infinite number of missing values between 0 and 1 which can be determined from the diagonal construction of Cantor. Since the values between 0 and 1 are continuous, there will be an infinite set of possibilities for even a single matrix element and the number of possible diagonals will be infinite. All this can happen for other matrix elements which can have any value between 0 and 1.

We note that (b) implies the satisfaction of certain specific preconditions before such events can occur. Some of these conditions would require to be quantized i.e., they are discrete and others continuous with each matrix element having many possible values.

Cardinality is used essentially to differentiate between discrete and continuous. We consider an actual example from atomic spectroscopy to apply the Continuum Theory to quantum mechanics.

It is known that there is a certain natural width ΔE_0 corresponding to an intensity distribution of a spectral line emitted by an atom.

In classical theory, this is due to the reaction force of the emitted radiation on the emitting source. In quantum mechanics, following the perturbation theoretic treatment due to Weisskopf and Wigner,[5] one gets a formula for ΔE_0 which is consistent with the time-energy uncertainty relation where ΔE_0 is interpreted as an estimate of the accuracy with which an energy level is known, as Δt is the lifetime of the excited state of the atom. The continuum of the line width thus co-exists with the discrete structure of the levels. At higher energies, the levels will begin to overlap and a continuum of non-enumerable infinite number of states will come into existence.

Let us assume that the ratio of the energy width in the continuum state, which is riding on the discrete structure and the energy of the level, is proportionate to the ratio of the number of discrete states (n) and the next cardinal number given by 2^n.

$$\text{i.e. } \rho \quad \frac{n}{2^n} = \frac{\Delta E_0}{E} \qquad \text{..................... (1)}$$

where ρ is some constant of conversion from cardinal states to energy states and $\Delta t \simeq \frac{h}{\Delta t}$ is the spread of the level of energy E and is related to the time and an atom can retain excess energy before re-emitting it in the form of photons.

We now apply the above formula to the case of a free electron falling to the various levels of the hydrogen atom. Table 1 gives the cardinal levels, the simplest series of the levels of the hydrogen atom and the energy widths.

TABLE 1: CARDINALITY AND THE WIDTH OF SPECTRAL LINES OF HYDROGEN FOR CONSTANT P

1 Card no.	*2* Quantum No.	*3* 2^n	*4* $\frac{n}{2^n}$	*5* E(ergs) Energy Level	*6* ΔE_0 Width (ergs)
1	8	2	0.500	3.37×10^{-13}	1.7×10^{-19}
2	7	4	0.500	4.39	2.2
3	6	8	0.375	5.99	2.2
4	5	16	0.250	8.61	2.2
5	4	32	0.156	13.45	2.1
6	3	64	0.094	24.00	2.25
7	2	128	0.055	53.90	3
8	1	256	0.031	214.00	6

The ratio of the values of $\frac{n}{2^n}$ and $\frac{\Delta E_o}{E}$ is nearly the same provided we allow for the variation of the value of ΔE_0. ρ is some constant which had to have the value of 10^6.

It will be noticed that the three levels which are nearer the ground state could belong to a separate family having a different cardinality. These first three levels could be of cardinality 3 which in turn can give rise to eight levels of higher cardinality.

From equation (1) it was shown that the natural width of the spectral lines of the hydrogen spectrum could be obtained using the Continuum Theory of Cantor. Here we show that the level spacing given by the theory is consistent with the Quantum Theory of the Hydrogen Atom.

Let D_1 be the level spacing of the hydrogen atom as given by the Bohr formula.

$$D_1 = \text{Const} \left[\frac{1}{p^2} - \frac{1}{q^2}\right] \qquad \ldots\ldots\ldots\ldots\ldots\ldots \qquad (2)$$

where ρ and q are the quantum numbers and the constant is the Rydberg constant. From equation (1) we have D_2 i.e.,

$$D_2 = \rho\left(\frac{n}{2^n} - \frac{m}{2^m}\right) = \Delta E_o\left(\frac{E_n - E_m}{E_m E_n}\right) \qquad \ldots\ldots\ldots\ldots\ldots\ldots \qquad (3)$$

Table 2 gives the values of D_1 & D_2. Here the cardinal number eight corresponds to the quantum number q=1, and the ordering of the cardinal numbers is in reverse order to the quantum numbers. The last column gives $\frac{\rho}{\Delta E_o}$

For $\rho = 1 \times 10^{-6}$ and cardinality 8 i.e., quantum number 1, $\Delta\lambda$ the spectral width comes out to be 1.17×10^{-4} ÅU, which is the value given by quantum mechanics.

It is known that the hydrogen lines are grouped in various series such as Lyman, Balmer, Paschen, etc. It therefore suggests that ρ and ΔE_0 need not necessarily be constant but can have quantized values. In Fig. 1, n/2En is plotted against -Log E. The degeneracy of the hydrogen lines makes it difficult to bring out the changes in the

TABLE 2: CARDINALITY AND THE BOHR THEORY OF THE HYDROGEN ATOM

1	2	3	4	5	6		7	8
n	$n-1-\left(\frac{n}{2^n}-\frac{n-1}{2^{n-1}}\right)\times 2^8$ $\left(=\frac{D_2}{\rho}\right)$		$E_n E_{n-1}$ $\times 10^{26}$	$(3)\times(4)$ $\times 10^{26}\times 2^8$	p	q	$D_1=-R_H hc\left(\frac{1}{p^2}-\frac{1}{q^2}\right)$ $\times 10^{12}$	$\frac{\rho}{\Delta E_\circ}\times 10^{-14}$ erg^{-1}
8	7	6	11615	69690	2	1	16.5	0.06
7	6	10	1293	12930	3	2	3.06	0.06
6	5	16	324	5184	4	3	1.07	0.052
5	4	24	116	2784	5	4	0.495	0.045
4	3	32	51.57	1650	6	5	0.269	0.041
3	2	32	26.29	841	7	6	0.162	0.049
2	1	0	14.93	0	8	7	0.105	–

value of ρ and $\Delta E_\circ$. But the changes in the slopes are clearly visible as we move from series to series.

Using the equations $\frac{\rho}{\Delta E_\circ} = 0.06\text{x}10^{14}$ (Table 2);

$\rho\frac{8}{2^8} = \frac{\Delta E_\varsigma}{E}$ $\frac{\Delta E_\circ}{E} = \frac{\Delta\lambda_\circ}{\lambda}$ where $\Delta\lambda_\circ$ is the natural line width, $\Delta\lambda_\circ = 1.17\text{x}10^{-4}$ ÅU and $E\lambda = hc$, ρ takes the value of $1\text{x}10^{-6}$.

This value establishes a consistency between Tables 1 and 2 and also establishes a consistency between the Bohr Theory of the Hydrogen Atom and the present work.

We now apply the Cantor Continuum Principle to another branch of physics which deals with elementary particles. Earlier, the energy levels of the hydrogen atom were considered because of the elementary nature of the particles involved, and the fact that the problem had been solved by quantum mechanics and could be used to compare the results of the two theories. The Theory of Elementary Particles concerns problems in the forefront of physics and a complete solution is far from complete. An attempt is made to derive some order in the distribution of masses of elementary particles as it is essentially a problem of energy levels. The Cantor Continuum Principle is so general that it can be used in principle to study all physical problems involving discreteness and continuity. It is not possible to apply the present theory to problems where there is close interaction between particles as in the case of nuclear

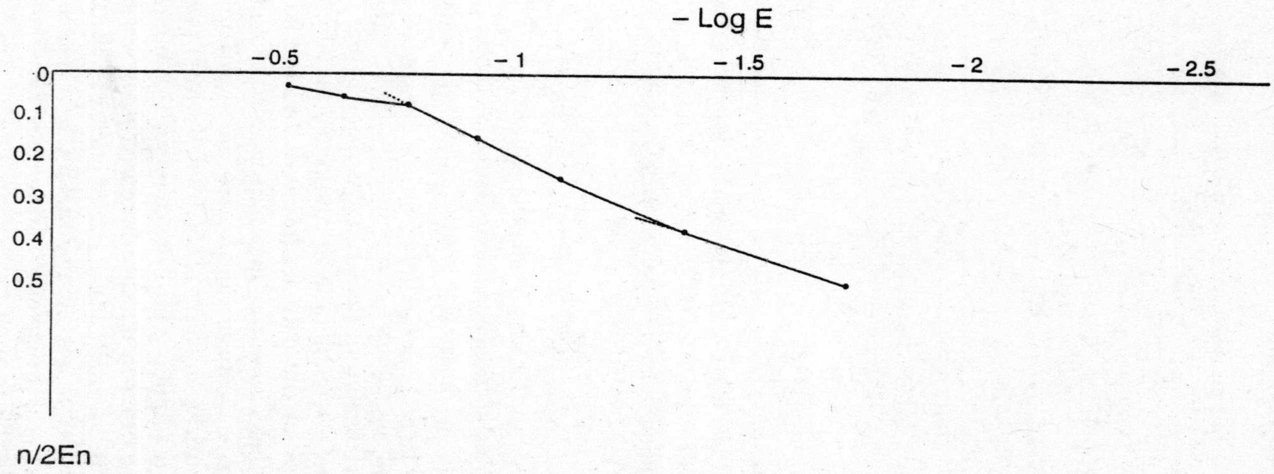

FIGURE 1

– Log E vs. n/2En showing the change in the values of ρ due to the formation of Lyman, Balmer and Paschen series. The change in the slopes are clearly visible.

physics, but it could stand a trial with isolated elementary particles.

If T_0 is the lifetime of an elementary particle, its energy width is given by h/T_0. If M is the mass of the particle in ergs and C is some constant, we have from equation 1

$$\Delta E_0/E = h/T_0M = C.\, n/2^n$$

Since we know from experimental data, the life-times of many of these particles and their masses, we can determine the values of $C.n/2^n$. By considering different values of the constant C and by selecting the values of the cardinal number for various values of C, it can be shown that for values of C=10E-1, C=10E-8 and C=10E-15, the values of log h/T M when plotted against log $n/2^n$ give straight lines. From Table 3 and Fig. 2, we can infer the following:

(a) It is possible to see some ordering among the masses and life-times of elementary particles through the choosing of an appropriate cardinal number.

(b) Though the choice of the cardinal number may seem arbitrary, the intercepts of the three lines grouping the particles divide them according to their life-times in the following manner:
 (1) Those whose life-times are between 1000 secs. and 10^{-8} sec.
 (2) Those whose life-times are between 10^{-10} sec. and 10^{-13} sec. and
 (3) Those whose life-times are beyond 10^{-17} sec. and 10^{-24} sec.

(c) It is seen from Fig. 2 and Table 3 that particles described as strange (Str.), charm (Chm.) and bottom (Bot.) are found in the sides of triangles ABC, CDE and FGI respectively. It suggests that ψ' should be a strange particle. All particles found at H are hyperons. One could expect new particles at points marked D, G and I.

(d) The cardinal number by itself represents the overlap of the continuous elements with the discrete elements as given by equation 1. For example, the neutron has a high cardinal number of 39. This means that it's discreteness and thus it's identity/reality is well-preserved. In the case of those with lower cardinal numbers, further investigation is required to see whether it is possible to connect their interactive proper-

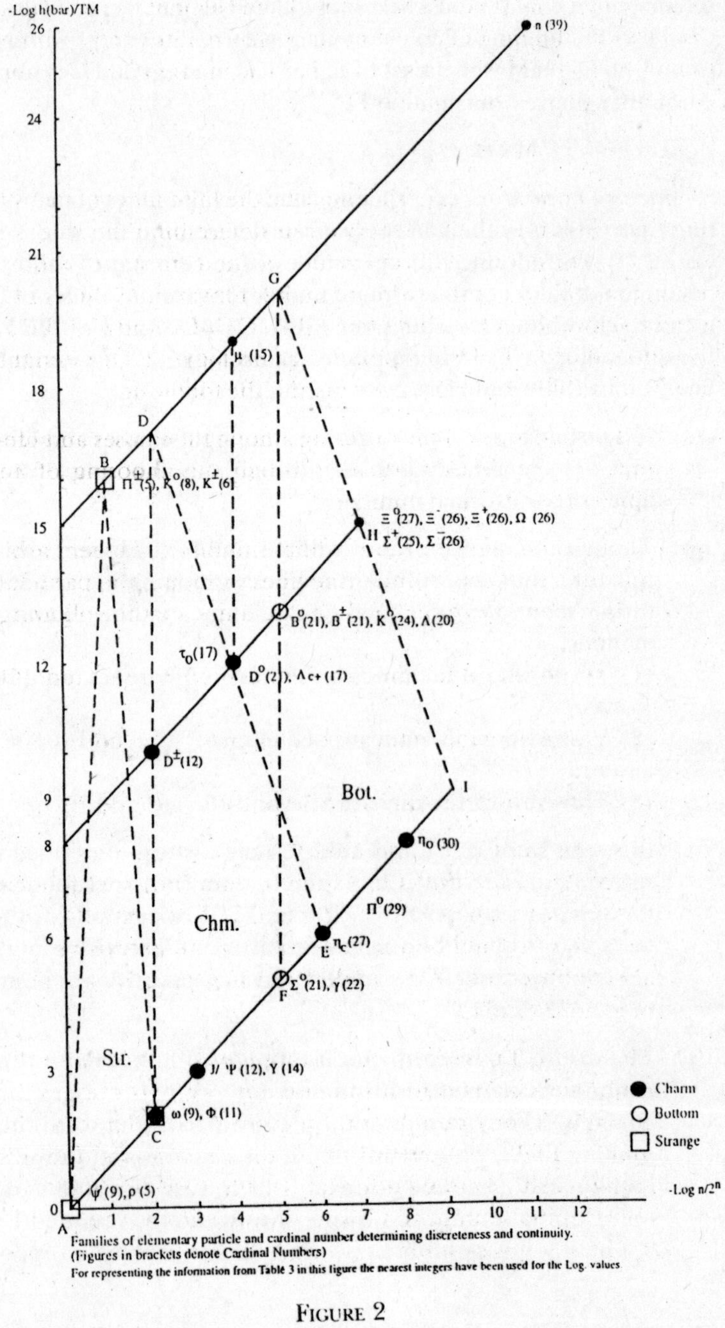

Families of elementary particle and cardinal number determining discreteness and continuity.
(Figures in brackets denote Cardinal Numbers)
For representing the information from Table 3 in this figure the nearest integers have been used for the Log. values

FIGURE 2

ties, implying that a high component of continuous elements implies a greater capability of interaction with other particles leading to a loss of its identity.

It is interesting to note that out of 32 particles, 23 of them fall at points where -Log10 n/2En (implying $-\text{Log}_{10} \frac{h}{TM}$) is a prime number. The association of sets of particles with prime numbers leads to a clustering of cardinal numbers around the prime number concerned. Thus, cardinal numbers between 5 & 8, 9 & 12,14 & 16, 21 & 24, 28 & 30 and 39 & 42 correspond to 1, 2, 3, 5, 7 and 11 respectively.

The significance of these fundamental connections is yet to be investigated.

REAL AND VIRTUAL EVENTS

We now associate all observable events with the possible sequence of conditions given by the matrix and associate all virtual events, which as we know are predicted by Quantum Theory, with an infinite number of the missing sequences i.e., those different from the diagonal elements of the matrix.

If all the observable physical events are described by the elements of the matrix and if all virtual events are associated with the missing sequences, which now form a set by themselves, it provides for a 'duality'. This arises because for every real event A, there is a virtual event A', opposite in character, since a one-to-one co-relation exists between A and A'. Every sequence in the missing set arises from an element denied in the diagonal set.

Whether the wave and particle nature of matter which are both observable are found in A or A' depends on whether events belong to either (A)'s or (A')'s respectively. It also depends on the validity of the Complementarity Principle of Bohr. If particle and wave behaviour are described as both belonging to A only, then the wave and particle property can be observed simultaneously which is contrary to that predicted by Bohr.[7] If one is from event set A and the other from set A', they will be mutually exclusive.

CONCLUSION

Thus, depending on how we interpret the sequences and the nature of the values of the matrix elements, different kinds of realities begin to emerge. The purpose of the paper is to show that from purely philosophical considerations, it is possible to examine the essential unity of reality including physical reality. We have shown that by using a matrix representing conditioned reality, it is possible to understand our notions of causality and aspects of relativity and quantum mechanics through the use of cardinality and the Continuum Theory of Cantor. In a sense it brings the foundations of physics closer to Godel's Theorem which can also be proved using Cantor's method.[8]

TABLE 3: CARDINALITY AND ORDERING OF ELEMENTARY PARTICLES
MESONS AND BARYONS

	1 *Particle*	2 *Mass(M)* *(in ergs)*	3 *Decay Time* *(T) (secs)*	4 *h(bar)/* *TM*	5 *n*	6 *n/2^n*	7 *C*
1.	$\Pi^{\pm}$ Pion	0.2243E-3	2.6E-08	1.8E-16	5	1.5E-1	E-15
2.	Π° Pion	0.216E-3	8.7E-17	0.56E-7	29	0.54E-7	E-0
3.	ρ Meson	1.232E-3	4.3E-24	0.198E-0	5	0.156E-0	E-0
4.	ω Meson	1.25E-3	0.67E-22	1.25E-2	9	1.82E-2	E-0
5.	μ Meson	0.169E-3	2.197E-6	2.98E-19	15	3.1E-4	E-15
6.	τ Meson	2.854E-3	0.3E-12	1.2E-12	17	1.3E-4	E-8
	Strange Particles						
7.	$K^{\pm}$ Kaon	0.789E-3	1.24E-8	1.07E-16	6	0.94E-1	E-15
8.	ϕ Meson	1.019E-3	1.5E-22	6.869E-3	11	5.0E-3	E-0
9.	K° Kaon	0.789E-3	5.2E-16	0.25E-16	8	0.31E-1	E-15
			or 8.9E-11	0.15E-19	24	1.43E-6	E-8
	Charm Particles						
10.	D° Meson	2.97E-3	4.4E-13	0.8E-12	21	1.29E-4	E-8
11.	$D^{\pm}$ Meson	2.99E-3	9.2E-13	0.38E-10	12	0.29E-2	E-8
12.	η_c Meson	0.876E-3	6.0E-18	0.2E-6	27	0.19E-6	E-0
13.	J/ψ Meson	3.097E-3	1.0E-20	3.4E-3	12	2.9E-3	E-0
14.	ψ' Meson	3.77E-3	0.26E-22	0.0107E-0	9	0.018E-0	E-0
	Bottom						
15.	$B^{\pm}$ Meson	8.43E-3	14.2E-13	0.88E-13	21	1.0E-5	E-8
16.	B° Meson	8.44E-3	14.2E-13	0.38E-13	21	1.0E-5	E-8
17.	γ Meson	15.13E-3	1.5E-20	0.46E-5	22	0.52E-5	E-0
18.	$\eta_{\circ}$ Meson	5.48E-3	6.0E-18	3.19E-8	30	2.79E-8	E-0
19.	n Neutron	1.504E-3	898	7.8E-26	39	7.0E-11	E-15

1		*2*	*3*	*4*	*5*	*6*	*7*
			HYPERONS				
20.	Λ	1.784E-3	2.6E-10	2.2E-13	20	1.91E-5	E-8
21.	Σ^+	1.902E-3	0.8E-10	6.9E-15	25	7.45E-7	E-8
22.	Σ°	1.907E-3	5.8E-20	0.9E-5	21	1.00E-5	E-0
23.	Σ	1.915E-3	1.48E-10	3.7E-15	26	3.8E-7	E-8
24.	Ξ°	2.103E-3	2.9E-10	1.7E-15	27	2.0E-7	E-8
25.	Ξ^-	2.113E-3	1.642E-10	3.0E-15	26	3.8E-7	E-8
26.	Ω	2.675E-3	0.822E-10	4.7E-15	26	3.8E-7	E-8
	Ξ^+						
27.	Λc^+	3.649E-3	2.3E-13	1.2E-12	17	1.29E-4	E-8

My thanks are due to Prof. B.V. Sreekantan for many useful discussions. I also thank Prof. C.V. Sundaram for his continued support and encouragement. My thanks are also due to Dr Dipankar Home for carefully going through the manuscript and making very valuable suggestions.

NOTES AND REFERENCES

1. F. Th. Stcherbatsky, *Buddhist Logic.* Oriental Books, New Delhi, 1984; originally printed in *Bibliotheca Buddhica Series,* 1930, Vol. 26, Parts 1 and 2.
2. R. Podolny, *Something Called Nothing—Physical Vaccum: What is it?.* Mir Moscow, 1986.
3. G. Zukav, *The Dancing Wu Li Masters: An Overview of the New Physics,* Bantam Books, New York, 1979; also see R. Weber, *Dialogues with Scientists and Sages: The Search for Unity,* Routledge & Kegan Paul, London; R. Ramanna, 'Scientific Philosophy with Reference to Buddhist Thought', Padmapani Lecture, Tibet House, New Delhi, 1992.
4. R. Courant and H. Robbins, *What is Mathematics? An Elementary Approach to Ideas and Methods,* Oxford University Press, 1978, pp. 84.
5. Hans Reichenbach, *The Philosophical Significance of the Theory of Relativity.* Open Court, 1969, pp. 287–312. Reprinted in Jefferson H. Weaver, *The World of Physics,* Vol. 3, Simon and Schuster, 1987, pp. 780–98.
6. W. Heitler, *The Quantum Theory of Radiation,* second edition, Oxford University Press, 1944.
7. P. Ghose, D. Home and G.S. Agarwal, 'An "Experiment to Throw More Light on Light": Implications', *Physics Letters* A, 168, No. 2, pp. 95–99.
8. H. Weyl, *Philosophy of Mathematics and Natural Science,* Princeton University Press, 1949; R. Ramanna, 'Foundations of Scientific Thought', *Science and Culture,* 35, No. 112, pp. 649–660.

5

Significance of the Veda in the Context of Indian Religion and Spirituality

KIREET JOSHI

I

The four Vedas (*Ṛg-Veda, Yajur-Veda, Sāma-Veda and Atharva-Veda*) are *saṁhitas*, collections or compilations of selections made by Veda Vyāsa. There was evidently at that time a larger body of compositions, and since they spoke of the old and new rishis[1] and of 'fathers' (*pitarah*), it may safely be inferred that there was at that time a tradition of generations of rishis. Presumably there was a pre-Vedic tradition too, since the Vedic compositions included in the four Vedas indicate a high level of development of poetic quality and spiritual experience, which can come about only through a long period of growth. It is difficult, however, to arrive at any conclusive determination of the dates of the Vedic or the pre-Vedic age, since there are varying opinions, and even conservative estimates vary between 5000 BC and 1500 BC.[2]

The name that was found by the Vedic rishis for their expressive words and hymns was *mantra*. According to Vedic theory, the spirit of creation framed all the movements of the world by *chhandas*, fixed rhythms of the formative word. The metrical movements of the Vedic *mantras* reflect these cosmic rhythms as powers of balanced harmonies maintained by a system of subtle recurrences. *Mantra* is poetic speech which combines three highest intensities: the intensity of rhythmic movement, of interwoven verbal form and thought-substance, and of the soul's vision of truth. *Mantra* is that rhythmic speech, which as the Veda puts it, rises at once from the heart of the seer and from the distant home of Truth. The Vedic poet is conscious of his poetic activity; he is consciously engaged in the process of the Yoga of Works and the Yoga of Knowledge, and, in this process, he goes beyond mere intellectual illuminativeness and discovers that more intense illumination of speech, that inspired word and supreme inevitable utterance, in which there meets the unity of a divine rhythmic movement with a depth of sense and a power of infinite suggestion welling up directly from the fountain-heads of the spirit. The resultant Vedic poetry is seen as an epic chant of the spirit, its struggle and delight of ascent and victory, the secret of which is contained in self-consecration and surrender of the finite to the infinite, a *yajña,* where knowledge, action and love meet and become one.

Vedic poetry is mystical and symbolic, and since the poets of the Veda were of a different mindset than ours, their use of images is of a peculiar kind and an antique cast of vision gives a strange outline to their substance. In their method, a fixed system of outward images is used as the body of the poetry, while freedom is often taken to pass their first limits, to treat them only as initial suggestions and transmute subtly or even cast them aside or subdue into a secondary strain or carry them out of themselves so that the translucent veil they offer to our minds lifts from or passes into open revelation.

In the eyes of the rishis, the physical and the psychical worlds were a manifestation and a two-fold and diverse and yet connected and similar figure of cosmic godheads, the inner and outer life of man a divine commerce with the gods, and behind was the one Spirit or Being of which the gods were names and personalities and powers, *ekam sat vipra bahudha vadanti.*[3] These godheads were not only masters of physical Nature but they were at the same time inward divine powers. Simultaneously also, they were states and energies born in our psychic being. Godheads, *devas,* are declared to be the guardians of truth and immortality, the children of the Infinite, and each of them to be in his origin and his last reality the supreme Spirit manifesting one of his aspects. In the Vedic vision, the life of man is a thing of mixed truth and falsehood, a movement from mortality to immortality, from mixed light and darkness to the splendour of a divine Truth whose home is above in the Infinite but which can be built up here in man's soul and life. This building up the home of Truth here implies a journey and a battle between the children of Light and the sons of Night, a getting of treasure, of the wealth, the booty given by the gods to the human warrior, and a journey and a sacrifice. The Vedic poets spoke of these things in a fixed system of images taken from Nature and from the surrounding life of the warlike, pastoral and agricultural Aryan people. And these images centred round the cult of fire and the worship of the powers of living Nature and the institution of sacrifice. The Vedic poets used for their expression a fixed and yet variable body of other images and a glowing web of myth and parable which expressed to the initiates a certain order of psychic experience and actual realities.

II

Yaska has spoken of several schools of interpretation of the Vedas. He has declared that there is a triple knowledge and therefore a triple meaning of the Vedic hymns, a sacrificial or ritualistic knowledge, a knowledge of the gods and finally a spiritual knowledge. He also says that the last is the true essence and when one gets it the others drop or are cut away. According to him, 'the rishis saw the Truth, the true law of things, directly by an inner vision'. He also said that 'the true sense of the Vedas can be recovered directly by meditation and *tapasya*'. We also find that the Vedic rishis themselves believe that their *mantras* contain a secret knowledge and that the words of the Veda could only be known in their true meaning by one who was himself a seer or mystic; from others the verses withhold their knowledge. For example, in *RV* IV.3.16, the rishi describes himself as one illumined, expressing through his thought and speech words for guidance, 'secret words'—*ninyā vachāmsi*—'wisdoms that utter their inner meaning to the seer'—*kāvyāni kavaye nivacanā.*[4]

The tradition of mystic elements in the Vedas has remained alive throughout the ages, and it is this tradition which is seen as the source of Indian civilization, its religion, philosophy, and culture.

It is, however, true that there was an external aspect of the Vedic religion and this aspect took its foundation in the mind of the physical man and provided means, symbols, rites, figures which were drawn from the most external things, such as heaven and earth, sun and moon and stars, dawn and day and night, rain and wind and storm, oceans and rivers and forests, and of the circumstances of the force of the vast and mysterious surrounding life. But even in its external aspect, Vedic religion spoke of a highest Truth, Right, Law of which the gods were the guardians, of the necessity of true knowledge and the larger inner life according to this Truth and Right, and of the home of immortality to which the soul of man could ascend by the power of truth and right being. In addition, Vedic religion provided sufficient ground to draw even common people in their ethical nature and to turn them towards some initial developments of their psychic being, and to conceive the idea of a knowledge and truth other than that of the physical life and to admit even a first conception of some greater spiritual Reality.

But the deeper and esoteric meaning of the Veda was reserved for the initiates, for those who were ready to understand and practise the inner sense. It was the inner meaning, it was the highest psychic and spiritual truth concealed by the outer sense that gave the Vedic hymns the name by which they are still known, the Veda, the Book of Knowledge. Only in the light of this esoteric sense can we understand the full flowering of the Vedic religion in the Upaniṣads and in the later development of Indian spiritual seeking and experience.

The inner Vedic religion attributes psychic significance to the godheads in the cosmos. It conceives of a hierarchical order of worlds, and an ascending stair of planes of being in the universe, *bhur, bhuvah, swar.* Truth and Right (*satyam* and *ritam*), which have their home in the highest world of *swar,* sustain and govern all the levels of Nature. They are one in essence but they take different forms at different levels of existence. For instance, there is in the Veda the series of the outer physical light, another higher and inner light which is a vehicle of the mental, vital and psychic consciousness, and a highest inmost light of spiritual illumination. Surya, the Sun-god, was the lord of the physical Sun, but he is at the same time the giver of the rays of Knowledge which illumine the mind, and he is also the soul of energy and the body of spiritual illumination.

All the Vedic godheads have an outer but also an inner and inmost basic principle, their known as well as secret names. All of them have various powers of some one highest reality, *ekam sat, tat satyam, tad ekam.* Each of these gods is in himself a complete and separate cosmic personality of the one Existence. And in their combination of powers they form the complete universal power, the cosmic whole. Each, again, apart from his special function, is one godhead with the others. Each holds in himself the universal divinity, each god is all the other gods. This complex aspect of Vedic teaching and worship has been given by the European scholar the title of henotheism. Beyond, there is, according to the Vedas, triple Infinite, and in this Infinite, the godheads put on their highest nature and are names of the one nameless Ineffable.

This teaching was applied to the inner life of man, and this application may be regarded as its greatest power. Power of the godheads can be built according to Vedic teaching, within man, and affirmation of these powers leads to the conversion of human nature into universality of divine nature. The gods are the guardians and increasers of the Truth, the powers of the Immortal, the sons of the Infinite Mother, Aditi. Man arrives at immortality by calling of the gods into himself by means of a connecting sacrifice, by surrender. This leads to the breaking of the limitations not only of his physical self but also of his mental and ordinary psychic nature. The Veda describes various experiences which indicate a profound psychological and psychic discipline leading to highest spiritual realization of divine status. This discipline contains the nucleus of the later Indian Yoga, its fundamental idea being the journey from the unreal to the real, from darkness to light, from death to immortality. The Vedic rishis speak of this as *ritasya panthā*, the path of the Truth. In one of the vivid descriptions of spiritual realization, Vāmadeva records: 'Vanished the darkness, shaken in its foundation; heaven shone out; upward rose the light of the divine Dawn; the sun entered the vast fields beholding the straight things and the crooked in mortals. Thereafter indeed they awoke and saw utterly; then indeed they held in them a bliss that is enjoyed in heaven, *ratnam dhārayanta dyubhaktam.* Let all the gods be in all our humans, let there be the truth of our thought, O Mitra, O Varuṇa'.[5] This is similar to another experience described by Parashara Shaktya, who declares: 'Our fathers broke open the firm and strong places by their words, yea, the *angirasas* broke open the hill by their cry; they made in us the path to the great heaven; they found the Day and *swar* and vision and the luminous Cows', *chakrur divo bṛhato gātum asme, ahah svar vividuh ketum usrāh.*[6] He declares again: 'They who enter into all things that bear right fruit formed a path towards the immortality; earth stood wide for them by the greatness by the Great Ones, the mother Aditi, with her sons came for the upholding'.[7]

These and other statements give us a clue to what the Vedic rishis meant by immortality. When the physical being is visited by the greatness of the infinite planes above and by the power of the great godheads who reign on those planes break its limits, open it out to the Light and is upheld in its new wideness by the infinite Consciousness, mother Aditi and her sons, the divine powers of the supreme *Deva*—then one realizes immortality.

Veda makes a distinction between the state of Knowledge and the state of Ignorance (*chittim achittim chinavad vi vidvān*), and discovers the means by which ignorance can be overcome. Upholding the thought of the truth in all the principles of our being, the diffusion of Truth in all parts of our being, and the birth of activity of all the godheads—this is the quintessence of the means of attaining Knowledge, which results in immortality.[8]

In the Veda we find the most characteristic ideas of Indian spirituality in their embryonic form. There is, first, the idea of the one Existence,[9] supra-cosmic, beyond the individual and universe. There is also the idea of one god who presents to us various forms, names, powers, personalities of his godhead. There is, thirdly, the distinction between Knowledge and Ignorance, the greater truth of an immortal life opposed to falsehood and mortal existence. Fourth, there is the conception of the discipline of an inward growth of man from the physical through the psychic to the spiritual existence. Finally, there is the idea and experience of the conquest of death, the secret of immortality. These ideas have remained constant in the Vedic tradition throughout its long and uninterrupted history upto the present day.

III

The Vedic beginning was a high beginning, and it was secured in its results by a larger sublime efflorescence. This is what we find in the Upaniṣads, which have always been recognized in India as the crown and end of the Veda, Vedānta. While the Brāhmaṇas[10] concentrated on the Vedic rituals, the Upaniṣads[11] renewed the Vedic truth by extricating it from its cryptic symbols and casting it into a highest and most direct and powerful language of intuition and experience. Indeed, this language was not the thing of the intellect, but still it wore a form which the intellect could take hold of, translate into its own more abstract terms and convert into a starting-point for an ever-widening and deepening philosophic speculation and reason's long search after the Truth.

The Upaniṣads are records of the deepest spiritual experience, and documents of revelatory and intituitive philosophy of an inexhaustible light, power and magnitude. Whether written in verse or cadenced prose, they are spiritual poems of unfailing inspiration, inevitable in phrase and wonderful in rhythm and expression. They are epic hymns of self-knowledge, and world-knowledge and God-knowledge. The imagery of the Upaniṣads is in large part developed from the type of imagery of the Veda. Ordinarily, it prefers unveiled clarity of directly illuminative image, but it frequently uses the same symbols in a way that is closely akin to the spirit of the older symbolism. The Upaniṣads are not a revolutionary departure from the Vedic mind but a continuation and development and to a certain extent an enlarging transformation. They simplify what was held covered in the symbolic Vedic speech as a mystery and a secret. Ajātaṣatru's explanation of sleep and dream, passages of the *Praśna Upaniṣad* on the vital being and its motion are some of the examples of Upaniṣadic symbolism.[12]

Along with the Veda, the Upaniṣads rank as *śruti,* since they embody revelations and intuitions of spiritual experience. The Upaniṣads are the acknowledged source of numerous profound philosophies and religions that flowed from them in India. They fertilized the mind and life of the people and kept India's soul alive through the centuries. Like a fountain of inexhaustible life-giving water, they have never failed to give fresh illumination. It is even being said that Buddhism was only a statement of one side of the Upaniṣadic experience, although it represented a new standpoint and provided fresh terms of intellectual definition and reasoning. Even in Pythagorian and Platonic thought, one could rediscover the ideas of the Upaniṣads. Sufism has been repeating the teaching of the Upaniṣads in another religious language. Even some of the modern thinkers of the East and the West seem to be absorbing the ideas of the Upaniṣads with living and intense receptiveness. And it may not be an exaggeration to say that there is hardly a main philosophical idea which cannot find an authority or a seed or an indication in those ancient and antique writings. It has also been claimed that the larger generalizations of science are found to apply to the truth of the physical Nature formulas which were discovered by the Upaniṣadic sages.

The Upaniṣads are Vedānta, a book of knowledge, but knowledge understood not as a mere thought process, but as a seeing with the soul and total living in it with the power of inner being, a spiritual seizing by a kind of identification with the object of knowledge. Through this process of knowledge by identity or intuition, the seers of the Upaniṣads came easily to see that the self in us is one with the universal self of all things and that this self again is the same as God and *Brahman*, a transcendent Being or Existence, and they beheld, felt, lived in the inmost truth of all things in the universe and the inmost truth of man's inner and outer existence by the light of this one and unifying vision.

Hence the three great declarations of the ancient Vedānta are: 'I am he',[13] 'Thou art That, O Swetaketu',[14] 'All this is the *Brahman*; this Self is the *Brahman*.[15]

The main conceptions of the Upaniṣads remained in parts in the various philosophical systems and efforts were made from time to time to reassemble them. Nyāya, Vaiśeṣika, Sāṁkhya, Yoga, Pūrva Mīmāṃsā and Uttara Mīmāṃsā bear the imprint of Upaniṣadic thought, and the last one, particularly has as its basic text, *Brahma-sūtra,* which was composed by Bādārayan, and in which the quintessence of the Upaniṣads was expounded aphoristically. *Brahma-sūtra* came to be commented upon by various Ācāryas. This gave rise to at least five schools of Vedāntic interpretation, viz., Advaita of Śaṅkarācārya, Viṣiṣṭādvaita of Rāmānujacārya, Viśuddhādvaita of Vallabhācārya, Dvaitādvaita of Nimbārkacārya, and Dāvaita of Madhvācārya. *Bhagwad Gītā* is also considered to be an exposition of the essence of the Upaniṣadic teaching. The commentary literature on the Upaniṣads, *Brahma-sūtra* and *Bhagwad Gītā*, continue to develop even in our present times.

It is true that the Upaniṣads are mainly concerned with the inner vision and not directly with outward human action; yet, all the highest ethics of Buddhism and later Hinduism are emergences of the very life and significance of the truths to which they give expressive form and force, and they even present the supreme ideal of a spiritual action founded on oneness with god and all living beings. It is for this reason that even when the life of the forms of the Vedic cult had passed away, the Upaniṣads still remained alive and creative and could generate the great devotional religions and inspire the persistent Indian idea of the *dharma*.

By the time we come to the Upaniṣads, the original Vedic symbols had begun to lose their significance and to pass into obscurity. The earlier stage of culture represented an old poise between the two extremes. On one side, there was the crude or half-trained naturalness of the outer physical man; on the other, there was an inner and secret psychic and spiritual life for the initiates. But this poise was disturbed because of the necessity of large-lined advance. The developing cycle of civilization called for a more and more generalized intellectual, ethical and aesthetic evolution. This called for a new order. At this juncture, the Upaniṣads saved the ancient spiritual knowledge by an immense effort, and the spiritual edifice created by the Upaniṣads guided, uplifted and more and more penetrated into the wide and complex intellectual, aesthetic, ethical and social culture that came to be developed in the post-Vedic age.

IV

During this post-Vedic age, which extended right upto the decline of Buddhism, we see the rise of the great philosophies, multifaceted epic literature, beginnings of arts and science, evolution of vigorous and complex societies, formation of large kingdoms and empires, manifold formative activities of all kinds and great systems of living and thinking. A number of scientific or systematic bodies of intellectual knowledge came up at an early stage. Actually, Vedāṅgas had begun to develop even before the Upaniṣads. *Māndukya Upaniṣad* mentions six Vedāṅgas; *śikṣa* (phonetics); *kalpa* (rituology); *vyākaraṇa* (grammar); *nirūkta* (etymology); *chhanda* (metrics); and *jyotiṣ* (astronomy and astrology). Each Vedāṅga takes up one aspect of the Veda and an attempt is made to explain it.

In due course, there developed a vast literature on these Vedāṅgas, expounding various systems of phonetics, rituals of sacrifices and rules of conduct of various kinds such as those described in *Śrauta-sūtra, Gṛihya-sūtra* and *Dharma-sūtra,* principles and details of Vedic etymology, grammatical subtleties, various forms, meters and styles of poetry, and several systems of astronomical and astrological knowledge. There also developed considerable literature of *pratiśākhya,* which dealt with the subtleties of grammar, meters and pronunciation pertaining to the *śākhas*[16] of the Vedas. Apart from the Vedāṅgas, there developed four sciences, known as Upavedas, viz., *Āyur-veda, Dhanur-veda, Gāndharva-veda* and *Artha-veda.* Here again, in due course, there developed a vast literature of expositions, commentaries and treatises.

Strong intellectuality of this period was inspired by the wide variety of spiritual experience and the synthetic turn so visible in the Vedas and the Upaniṣads. There was conscious perception that spiritual experience is higher than religion and that what religion seeks can really be attained by the inner psychological discipline, which in due course came to be developed into a *śāstra*, the *śāstra* of Yoga. This allowed intellectuality to become free from the crippling effects of religious dogma, and we find that the intellectual development became multi-sided. Materialistic atheism, agnosticism, scepticism, too developed. Indeed, this intellectuality was austere and rich, robust and minute, powerful and delicate, massive in principle and curious in detail. The mere mass of the intellectual production during the period from Ashoka well into the Muhammadan epoch is something scholarship gives of it. And while evaluating this account it must be noted that what has been dealt with so far of this ancient treasure is a fraction of what is still lying extant and what is extant is only a small percentage of what was once written and known. And we have also to note that what was accomplished had for its aid the power of memory and the perishable palm-leaf. The colossal literature extended to various domains,—philosophy and theology, religion and yoga, logic and rhetoric, grammar and linguistics, poetry and drama, medicine and astronomy and the sciences. It dealt also with politics and society, music and dancing, architecture and painting, all the sixty-four accomplishments, and various crafts and skills. It may be said that even such subjects as the breeding and training of horses and elephants had their own *śāstras*. Each domain of thought and life had a systematic body of knowledge, its art, its apparatus of technical terms, its copious literature.

During this period, India stood first in the fields of mathematics, astronomy, chemistry, medicine, surgery and all the branches of physical knowledge which were practised in ancient times. In many fields, India was ahead in discovery. It is true that the harmony that was established between philosophical truth and truth of psychology and religion was not extended in the same degree to the truth of physical nature. But from the beginning, starting from the thought of the Veda, the Indian mind had recognized that the same general laws and powers hold in the spiritual, psychological and physical existence. Omnipresence of life was discovered, and there was the affirmation of the evolution of the soul in Nature from the vegetable and the animal to the human form.

The philosophic mind started from the data of the spiritual experience, and it went back always in one form or another to the profound truth of the Veda and the Upaniṣad which kept their place as the highest authority in these matters. There was a constant admission that spiritual experience is a greater thing and its light a truer if more incalculable guide than the clarities of the reasoning intelligence. In the epic literature of the Mahābhārata and the Rāmāyana, we find a strong and free intellectual and ethical thinking; there is an incessant criticism of life by the intelligence and ethical reason. We find in it curiosity and desire to fix the norms of truth in all fields. But in the background there is a constant religious and spiritual sense and an implicit or explicit ascent to spiritual truth. In the field of art, there was insistence upon life and its creativity, but still its highest achievement was always in the field of the interpretation of the religio-philosophical mind. The whole tone of art during that period was coloured by a suggestion of the spiritual and the infinite.

The master ideas of the Vedas and the Upaniṣads governed the developing turn of imagination, its creative temperament and the kind of significant forms in which it persistently interpreted its perception of self and things and life and universe. The sense of the infinite and the cosmos generated by the Vedic hymns is seen in a great part of the literature of the subsequent ages also as we see it in architecture, painting and sculpture. As in the Veda, even so here, there is a tendency to see and render spiritual experience in images taken from the inner psychic plane or in physical images transmitted by the stress of a psychic significance and impression. The tendency to mirror the terrestrial life (often magnified), as in the Mahābhārata and in the Rāmāyana, reflects the Vedic influence.

On the front of community life, Indian society developed its communal co-ordination of the mundane life of interest and desire, *kāma* and *artha*. But it governed its action always by a reference at every point to the moral and religious law, the *dharma*, and it never lost sight of spiritual liberation, *mokṣa*, as the highest motive and ultimate aim of the effort of life. At a still later stage, when there came about an immense development of the mundane intelligence and an emphatic stress on aesthetic, sensuous and hedonistic experience, there was a corresponding deepening of the intensities of psycho-religious experience. It may be said that every excess of emphasis on the splendour and richness and power and pleasure of life had its asceticism. And throughout this development one can see the inner continuity with the Vedic and Vedāntic origins.

It is true that at one time it seemed as if a discontinuity would take place. Buddhism seemed to reject all spiritual continuity with the Vedic religion. Buddhism seemed also to signal a new beginning. But the ideal of *nirvāna* came to be perceived as a negative and exclusive statement of the highest Vedāntic spiritual experience. The eight-fold path also came to be perceived as an austere sublimation of the Vedic notion of the Right, Truth, and Law, which was followed as the way to immortality. The strongest note of Mahāyāna Buddhism, which laid a stress on universal compassion and fellow-feeling was seen as an ethical application of the spiritual unity which is an essential idea of Vedānta. The Buddhistic theory of *karma* could have been supported from the utterances of the Brāhmaṇas and the Upaniṣads. Actually, the Vedic tradition absorbed all that it could of Buddhism, but rejected its exclusive positions.

But there was a gradual fading out of the prominent Vedic forms and substitution of others. Symbol, ritual and ceremony were transformed; the lofty heights of the Vedic spiritual experience did not reappear as a predominant tendency, although there was a further widening and fathoming of psychic and spiritual experience. The Vedic pantheon gradually faded out altogether under the weight of the increasing importance of the great trinity, Brahma–Vishnu–Shiva. A new pantheon appeared; its outward symbolic aspect expressed a deeper truth and larger range of experience, feeling and idea. The tradition of the Vedic sacrifice began to break down; the house of Fire was replaced by the temple. The devotional temple ritual came to replace to a great extent the *karmik* ritual of sacrifice. More precise conceptual forms of the two great deities, Vishnu and Shiva, came to replace the vague and shifting mental images of the Vedic gods. The *śaktis* of Vishnu and Shiva also came to dominate the religious scene. These new concepts became stabilized in physical images, and these images were made the basis both for internal adoration and for external worship.

The esoteric teachings of the Vedic hymns which centred on the psychic and spiritual discipline disappeared, although some of its truths reappeared in various new forms. These forms as we see them in the Purāṇic and Tāntric religion and Yoga were less luminous than the Vedic nucleus of spiritual experience, but they were more wide and rich and complex and more suitable to the psycho-spiritual inner life.

The Purāṇo-Tāntric[17] stage was marked by an effort to awaken the inner mind even in the common man, to lay hold on his inner vital and emotional nature, to support all by an awakening of the soul and to lead him through these things towards a higher spiritual truth. This effort required new instruments, new atmosphere and new fields of religious and spiritual experience. While the Vedic godheads were to the mass of their worshippers divine powers who presided over the workings of the outward life of the physical cosmos, the Purāṇic Trinity had, even for the multitude, a predominant psycho-religious and spiritual significance. But the central spiritual truth remained the same in both the Vedic and Purāṇo-Tāntric systems, the truth of the one in many aspects. As the Vedic godheads were forms of the Supreme, even so the Purāṇic Trinity was a triple form of the one supreme Godhead and *Brahman*; even the *śaktis* were energies of the One Energy of the highest divine Being. But this truth was no longer reserved for the initiated few; it was now more and more brought powerfully, widely and intensely home to the general mind and feeling of the people.

The system of the hierarchy of the worlds that we find in the Veda was more intricate than the system we find in the Purāṇas. In the Veda, the highest worlds constitute the triple divine principle; infinity is their scope, bliss is their foundation. These three worlds are supported by the vast region of the Truth whence a divine Light radiates out towards our mentality in the three heavenly luminous worlds of *swar*, the domain of Indra. Below is the triple system in which we live. This triple system consists of three earths, three heavens, *dyaus*, and the connecting mid-region (*antarikṣa*). In simpler terms, the triple lower world in which we live is the world of matter, life-force and pure mind. According to the Vedic idea, each principle can be modified by the subordinate manifestation of the others within it, and each world is divisible into several provinces. Into this framework the Vedic rishis placed all the complexities of the subtle vision and fertile imagery. The Purāṇic system is a continuation of the Vedic system, but it is simpler. The Purāṇa recognizes seven principles of existence and the seven Purāṇic worlds correspond to them with sufficient precision, thus:

	Principle	*World*
1.	Pure Existence—*Sat*	World of the highest truth of being (*Satyaloka*)
2.	Pure Consciousness—*Cit*	World of infinite Will or conscious force (*Tapoloka*)
3.	Pure Bliss—*Ānanda*	World of creative delight of existence (*Janaloka*)
4.	Knowledge or Truth—*Vijñāna*	World of vastness (*Maharloka*)
5.	Mind	World of light (*Swar*)
6.	Life (nervous being)	World of various becoming (*Bhuvar*)
7.	Matter	The material world (*Bhur*)

The Vedic interpretation of life as a movement of sacrifice and a battle continued in the Purāṇo-Tāntric tradition also. According to the Veda, the struggle of life is a warring of Gods and the Titans, Gods and the Giants, Indra and the Python, Aryan and the Dasyu. In the Purāṇas and Tantras also, life is conceived as a struggle and battle between Devas and Asuras, Devas and Rākṣasas, between the armies of Gods and Goddesses and the armies of Āsuric, Rākṣasic and Paiśāchik adversaries. The Vedic goal of achieving immortality recurs also in the Purāṇas and Tantras, where we have symbolic story of the search after the nectar.

The Vedic idea of the divinity in man was popularized during the Purāṇo-Tāntric stage to an extraordinary extent; there was a development of the concept of *avatars*, of the occasional manifestations of the divine in humanity; there was also the development of the idea of the Divine Presence, discoverable in the heart of every creature. New systems of yoga also developed, but the basis was the same, namely, secret of the object of concentration, of the method of concentration, and of the object of concentration. There was, however, a many-sided endeavour which opened the gates of Yoga on various levels and planes of consciousness. Many kinds of psycho-physical, inner vital, inner mental and psycho-spiritual methods came to be developed; but all of them had the common aim of the realization of a greater consciousness and a more or less complete union with the One and Divine, or else an emergence of the individual soul in the Absolute. The Purāṇo-Tāntric system provided a basis of generalized psycho-religious experience from which man could rise through knowledge, works or love or through any other fundamental power of his nature of some supreme experience and highest or absolute status.

V

After the Purāṇo-Tāntric stage, there came the third stage of the development of religion and spirituality in India. The first stage consisted of the Vedic training of the physically minded man;[18] the second stage took up man's outward life as also a deeper mental and psychical life, and it brought man more directly into contact with the spirit and divinity within him. But now in the third stage, there was an attempt to take up man's whole mental, psychical, physical living so as to arrive at a first beginning at least of a generalized spiritual life. This is what we see after the decline of Buddhism in the emergence of the great spiritual movement of the saints and *bhaktas* and an increasing resort to various paths of yoga. During this stage, there was also a great problem of receiving Islam, and two great attempts were made to arrive at a new synthesis; one from the side of the Muslims, and the other from the side of the Hindus. The former was exemplified in the attempt of Akbar to create a new religion called *Din-Illahi*, and the latter was exemplified by the life and works of Guru Nanak. The work of Guru Nanak gave rise to the subsequent Sikh Khalsa movement which was astonishingly original and novel. During this period, there was a tremendous churning of the spirit of India, and a great attempt was made to explore all aspects of human beings and to develop them in such a way that they could all open up to the spiritual light and force. This attempt had not only an individual aspect but also a collective aspect. This was a remarkable attempt which could have revolutionized the collective life of India. But this was interrupted on account of several factors.

Among these factors was the fact of the exhaustion of the vital force as a result of a long march and effort from the earliest times of Indian history. This exhaustion was also due to the fact that since the sixth century BC there entered a current of culture which negated the meaning and the significance of cosmic life. This created confusion and imbalance resulting in excessive asceticism. It impoverished life and led to the neglect of social, economic and political conditions of the country. High ideals began to be exiled from active life, and rigidities of various kinds came to imprison the forms of individuals and collectivities. The exhaustion of vital force in the country coincided also with the political instability and the coming of the settlers from the West. Finally, the establishment of the British supremacy in India resulted in the extreme impoverishment of the Spirit of India.

VI

The third stage of religious and spiritual development of India could not bear its natural fruit, although it has done much to prepare a great possibility for the future. The message of the third stage is that the spiritualization of the collective life cannot be achieved if only the physical mind of man is trained or even if a greater effort is made to train the psychic-emotional part of man's nature. What is needed is to turn the entirety of mental, psychical and physical living of the individual and the collectivity to divinize the whole of human life and nature. It is significant, therefore, to note that there arose from the middle of the nineteenth century a reassertion of the Indian spirit, and this reassertion is marked by three tendencies, namely, re-affirmation of the spiritual ideal, emphasis on dynamism and creative action, and insistence on collective domains and forms of life. At the beginning of this period there arose a galaxy of great personalities, like Raja Rammohun Roy and Dayanand Saraswati, Sri Rama Krishna and Swami Vivekananda, who filled India with a new breath and sowed the seeds not only of a spiritual awakening but also of social and political awakening. The new nationalist spirit was at once spiritual and social in character, and it symbolized a new vibration.

It is significant also that in this new awakening, the Veda and the Upaniṣads were rediscovered. The esoteric teaching of the Vedas which was confined only to initiates during the Vedic period, in the new light seemed to be a store from which we all can even now draw illumination and power of regeneration. The new light does not advocate a mere revival or a prolongation of the Purāṇic system by points to something which the Vedic seers saw as the aim of human life and which the Vedāntic sages cast into the clear and immortal forms of the luminous revelation. And yet it is not to the Vedic forms that we are called upon to return. The great message of modern India, coming through its accomplished rishi, Śri Aurobindo, calls for the discovery of newer light and development of newer forms. Not to trace or retrace the old, but taking into account the treasures of the past and by liberating or developing new knowledge, even by hewing new paths we are called upon to find original solutions to build up a new centre of spiritual consciousness which can manifest that consciousness potently in all fields of activity, scientific, philosophical, cultural, social, economic, political.

VII

Significance of the Veda is not confined merely to the fact that it is the world's first yet extant scripture, but that it is the earliest interpretation of Man and the Divine and Universe as also that it is a sublime and powerful poetic creation. The utterances of the greatest seers, Viśwamitra, Vāmadeva, Dirghatamas and many others touch the most extraordinary heights of *māntric* poetry. At the early stages of the Vedic tradition, the substance of Indian religion and spirituality came to be determined by the variety of deep psychic and spiritual experiences shared and expressed by hundreds of the Vedic seers. It can be seen that the post-Vedic and later spirituality of the Indian people was contained in the Veda in seed or in first expression.

A great force of intuition and inner experience, so evident in the Veda and the Upaniṣad, gave to the Indian mind the sense and reality of cosmic consciousness and cosmic vision. Perception of the One underlying reality, recognition of the perception of unity, as *vidyā*, and the necessity of the individual to lift himself from *avidyā* to *vidyā*—these are the connecting threads of Indian religion and spirituality, and these we see repeatedly emphasized in Vedic teaching. At the same time, we have to note that even while admitting the One without a second, *ekam eva advitiyam,* there was no paralyzing exclusion in the Veda and Upaniṣad, and there was a clear admission of the duality of the one and the distinction of the Spirit and Nature; and there was room also for various trinities and other aspects of that One, *tad ekam.* This has created in the Indian mind an aversion to intolerant and mental exclusions, and even when it concentrates sometimes on single limiting aspect of the Divinity—and seems to see nothing but that,—it still keeps instinctively at the back of its consciousness the sense of the All and the idea of the One. Even when it distributes its worship among many objects, it looks at the same time through the object of worship and sees beyond the multitude of godheads the Unity of the Supreme. What is of special significance is that this synthetic turn is not limited to the mystics or to philosophic thinkers, but it extends even to the popular mind, which has been permeated by the force of the thoughts, images, traditions and cultural symbols not only of the Veda and Vedānta but also of the Purāṇa and Tantra. There is in the Indian mind a pervasive synthetic monism, many-sided unitarianism, and large cosmic universalism.

This is not to deny the fact that there have emerged in the long course of Indian history tendencies, thoughts and even religious movements characterized by exclusivism. There have been exclusive claims and counter-claims and even quarrels and intolerance. But the efforts at synthesis have tended to prevail. Even in the field of philosophy, while trenchant positions are not absent, synthetic turn eventually predominates. In the field of Yoga, too, there have been specializations and exclusive claims and counter-claims; claims of the path of knowledge have opposed the claims of the path of action and devotion and vice-versa; but there have been powerful systems of the synthesis, such as those of the esoteric Veda, Upaniṣads, *Gītā* and Tantra. Even in later times, in the movements of saints and bhaktas there is a marked turn towards synthesis, and even in our own times, in the yogic life of Sri Aurobindo's integral yoga we have the latest effort and statement of the synthesis of yogic disciplines.

Catholicity of the Veda and the Upaniṣads has changed remarkably in the forms of Indian religion and spiritual culture, even while maintaining the persistence of their spirit. And if we examine the changes that have occurred, we shall find in them a meaningful process of evolution and a certain kind of logic. Right from the Vedic times, there was a tendency in Indian religion to provide means for the individual and collective life to develop by graded steps and reach and experience truths of higher and spiritual existence. It was recognized that at the beginning not many could safely and successfully reach the heights, but the pioneering leaders did not accept the theory that many must necessarily remain forever on the lower rungs of life and only a few climb into the free air and the light, but they were moved by the spirit to regenerate the totality of physical life on earth. It is true that this spirit was not at all times and in all its parts consciously aware of its own total significance. But the total drift of the manifold sides and rich variations of the forms, teachings and disciplines of Indian religion and spirituality indicate that the aim pursued was not only to raise to inaccessible heights the few elect, but to draw all men and all life and the whole human race upward, to spiritualize life and in the end to divinize human nature.

Indian spirituality, as seen in the Veda, recognized both the spiritual and physical poles of existence, and sought the experiences and realization of higher planes of the spirit even in physical consciousness (*prithvi*). The legend of the *angiras* rishis indicates the effort to discover the lost sun and herds of light in the caves of darkness, symbolizing physical inconscience. It may even be said that the Yoga of the Veda seems to suggest that the discovery of the light in Sūrya Savitri is followed and completed by the discovery and uncovering of the light in the very depths of darkness of the Inconscient, *tamas*. Not the rejection of matter and material life but realization that the matter too is spirit and that material life too can bear and manifest the spiritual light and bliss—this seems to be the inner basis of Vedic teaching.

It is this unitive perception that could explain the drift of Indian religion and spirituality towards a wide and many-sided culture. It is true that on its more solitary summits, at least in its later periods, Indian spirituality tended to a spiritual exclusiveness, which was, whatever its loftiness, quite impressive and excessive. Actually this exclusiveness imposed on Indian culture a certain impotence to deal effectively with the problems of human existence; consequently, there came about a general decline in science, philosophy, and in all other domains of life. On the other hand, the previous training provided by Vedic religion to the physically-minded early common man and by the post-Vedic and Purāṇo-Tāntric religion to the common man of the later periods who developed increasingly his intellectual, ethical, aesthetic, imaginative, emotional and vital faculties had created favourable conditions for the growth and development of multi-sided religious and spiritual movement that attempted to synthesize conflicting tendencies and to invite larger and larger sections of the society to the possibilities of the multi-sided spiritual training and development. Even though there was a general arrest of the new development, the Indian Renaissance had by now provided fresh conditions, and the most conscious and potent expression of the new spirituality had declared the aim not of individual salvation but of collective salvation. It has rejected the exclusive solution of the problems of human life in the attainment of world-negating spirit; it has rather affirmed the possibility of the highest spiritualizing of life on earth.

The earliest preoccupation of India, as expressed in the Veda, was the exploration of the spirit in matter and of matter in spirit; the intermediate preoccupation was with the seeking and experiment in a thousand ways of the soul's outermost and innermost experience marked by various conflicts and even exclusive affirmations and denials under an over-arching tendency towards multi-sided development of the spiritual, ethical, intellectual, aesthetic, vital and physical parts of the being and some kind of synthesis. The latest trend takes up the burden and treasure of the gains of the past and looks towards the future with some kind of basis of effective realization where tasks of the establishment of divine life on earth for full participation by the entire human race could be undertaken.

While outlining these tasks, particularly of the renascent India, Śri Aurobindo states:

> The recovery of the old spiritual knowledge and experience in all its splendour, depth and fullness is its first, most essential work; the flowing of this spirituality into new forms of philosophy, literature, art, science and critical knowledge is the second; an original dealing with modern problems in the light of Indian spirit and the endeavour to formulate a greater synthesis of a spiritualized society is the third and most difficult. Its success on these three lines will be the measure of its help to the future of humanity.[19]

NOTES AND REFERENCES

1. See, for example, *RV* I. 1.2.
2. According to Shri A.C. Das, the Vedas could have been composed any time between 259–750 BC. According to Lokamānya Tilak, the estimated period would be any time between 45–50 BC. This coincides with the view of Professor Haug, Professor Ludwig and Professor Jacobi. Professor Whitney places the period any time between 15–20 BC. Professor Max Müller believes that the Veda was composed during the thirteenth century BC.
3. *RV* I.164.46.
4. See also *RV* I.164.39, *RV* I.164.46; *RV* X.71.
5. *RV* IV.1.17.
6. *RV* I.71.3.
7. *RV* 1.72.9.

8. See also *RV* I.68. I–3.
9. Triple Infinite of the Veda, which was formulated as Sachchidānanda in the Upaniṣad.
10. The Brāhmaṇas contain detailed analysis of various categories of sacrifices, their rituals and procedures. They include also collections of history, legends, anecdotes and narrations of stories connected with individuals. The important Brāhmaṇas are : *Aitareya Brāhmaṇa, Śatapatha Brāhmaṇa, Taittirīya Brāhmaṇa, Kāthaka Brāhmaṇa, Jaiminīya Brāhmaṇa* and *Gopatha Brāhmaṇa.* A large number of Brāhmaṇas have been lost.
11. In the *Muktopaniṣad* it is mentioned that the total number of Upaniṣads is 108, and they are derived from the four Vedas. The Upaniṣads laid down the process of realisation of the *Brahman,* the ultimate Reality, which begins with the *Brahmajijñāsa,* aspiration to know the *Brahman* and it continues through the hearing of the Upaniṣads, reflection on the Upaniṣads and dwelling on the Upaniṣads. Important Upaniṣads are: *Aitareya, Māṇdukya* and *Kauṣītaki,* which are related to *Ṛgveda; Taittirīya, Katha* and *Śwetaṣvatara* which are related to *Kṛṣṇa Yajurveda; Brihadāraṇyaka* and *Īśā,* which are related to *Śukla Yajurveda; Kena* and *Chāndogya,* which are related to *Sāmaveda;* and *Praśna* and *Muṇdaka,* which are related to *Atharvaveda.*
12. We may also refer to the passage of the *Taittirīya* in which Indra appears as a power of the divine mind. The passage of the *Praśna Upaniṣad* may also be referred to where the power and the significance of the mystic syllable *AUM* are described.

    As an example of greater clarity of statements, which are nearer to our intellectual apprehension, we may refer to the passages of the *Katha Upaniṣad,* where the knowledge of the *Puruṣa,* no bigger than a thumb, as man's central self is given.
13. *Chāndogya Upaniṣad* : 4.11.1.
14. Ibid., 6.8.7.
15. Ibid., 3.14.1; also *Brihadāraṇyaka Upaniṣad*: 2.5.19.
16. The tradition of transmission of the recitation of the *Saṁhitās* gave rise to various recensions or *śākhas.* The total number of *śākhas* in the ancient period was 1131; but at present only 10 *śākhas* exist.
17. According to the tradition, the word Purāṇa is so-called because it is supposed to refer to the most ancient knowledge. It is said that Brahma had received the knowledge containing the Purāṇas from the Supreme Divine; Brahma transmitted it to his four mind-born sons, one of whom Sanat Kumara transmitted it to Nārada, who, in turn, transmitted it to Krishna Dwaipāyana, Veda Vyāsa. Veda Vyāsa composed that knowledge in 18 books, each one of them is called Purāṇa. There are also a number of Upapurāṇas. Purāṇas describe the creation of the universe, development of the universe, and the dissolution of the universe. Apart from many legends, Purāṇas contain ideas relating to birth, death and the condition of the soul after the death of the body. They also deal with questions relating to philosophic and yogic matters. Most importantly, Purāṇas are related to great deities, particularly Brahma, Vishnu and Shiva. An important contribution of the Purāṇa is related to the concept of divine incarnation, *avatāra.*

    The texts connected with tantra are numerous, probably sixty-four or even more. The tantric treatise is generally in the form of a dialogue between Shiva and his consort and it teaches mystical formulae for the worship of the deities or the attainment of superhuman powers. The *tantric yoga* is a kind of synthesis of yogic practices contained not only in *Karma yoga, Jñāna yoga,* and *Bhakti yoga* but also in *Mantra yoga, Hatha yoga* and *Raja yoga*. The tantric synthesis attempts to emphasize the notion of the divine perfectibility of man, which was also in Vedic teaching, but which was overshadowed in the intermediate ages.

18. We are not considering here the esoteric teaching of the Veda, which was limited only to the initiates, and which addressed itself to intellectual, vital and physical aspects of training also.
19. 'The Foundations of Indian Culture', Vol.14 of the Centenary Collection, p. 409.

Contributors

PRAJIT K. BASU is Assistant Professor in the Department of Humanities and Social Sciences, Indian Institute of Technology, New Delhi.

SIBAJIBAN BHATTACHARYYA, formerly Professor of Philosophy at different universities and institutions in India and abroad, is currently a National Fellow of the Indian Council of Philosophical Research (ICPR).

MAHESH TIWARY is a Professor in the Department of Buddhist Studies, University of Delhi.

RAJA RAMANNA, formerly Chairman of the Atomic Energy Commission, is currently Director of the National Institute of Advanced Studies, Bangalore.

KIREET JOSHI, formerly Special Secretary in the Department of Education, Ministry of Human Resource Development, is currently Chairman of the Value Education Centre and President of the Dharam Hinduja International Centre of Indic Research, Delhi.